WITHDRAWN

Audrey Fenner
Editor

Integrating
Print and Digital Resources
in Library Collections

Integrating Print and Digital Resources in Library Collections
has been co-published simultaneously as *The Acquisitions
Librarian*, Numbers 35/36 2006.

*Pre-publication
REVIEWS,
COMMENTARIES,
EVALUATIONS . . .*

"THOUGHT-PROVOKING. . . .
An interesting mix of case studies and research reports from working librarians in a variety of settings.
Librarians confounded by questions
about the print/digital mix–most of
us–will find in this book confirma-
tion of the dilemmas they have been
wrestling with, and alternative points
of view to consider."

Dana Hendrix, MALS
*Head
Collection Development and Acquisition
Smith Library Center
Southwestern University*

D0162478

More pre-publication
REVIEWS, COMMENTARIES, EVALUATIONS . . .

"**R**EQUIRED READING FOR LIBRARY AND INFORMATION SCIENCE STUDENTS, especially those interested in becoming serials specialists. . . . Presents various issues in managing print and electronic library resources, and providing access to them through the library's catalog and Web site. Chapters cover licensing, consortial purchasing, usage statistics, staff training, maintenance and cancellation of journal subscriptions, cataloging, and integrating access to all formats both in the library's catalog and the stacks."

Arlene Hanerfeld, MLS
*Associate University Librarian
for Technical and Collection Services
Randall Library
University of North Carolina Wilmington*

The Haworth Information Press
An Imprint of The Haworth Press, Inc.

Integrating
Print and Digital Resources
in Library Collections

Integrating Print and Digital Resources in Library Collections has been co-published simultaneously as *The Acquisitions Librarian*, Numbers 35/36 2006.

Monographic Separates from *The Acquisitions Librarian*™

For additional information on these and other Haworth Press titles, including descriptions, tables of contents, reviews, and prices, use the QuickSearch catalog at http://www.HaworthPress.com.

Integrating Print and Digital Resources in Library Collections, edited by Audrey Fenner (No. 35/36, 2006). *Examines the formats and technologies involved in combining print and electronic materials to form a thoroughly integrated library collection.*

Managing Digital Resources in Libraries, edited by Audrey Fenner (No. 33/34, 2005). *A practical guide to managing library materials in digital formats; examines innovations including the integration of PDA-accessible resources into collections and the developmnet of all-digital libraries.*

Selecting Materials for Library Collections, edited by Audrey Fenner (No. 31/32, 2004). *A comprehensive overview of building, maintaining, and updating any library collection.*

Collection Development Policies: New Directions for Changing Collections, edited by Daniel C. Mack (No. 30, 2003). *An in-depth guide to building and maintaining effective policy statements.*

Acquisitions in Different and Special Subject Areas, edited by Abulfazal M. Fazle Kabir (No. 29, 2003). *Presents profiles, methods, and processes for acquisitions in specialized subject areas, including local and regional poetry, oceanography, educational information in electronic formats, popular fiction collections, regional and ethnic materials, and more.*

Strategic Marketing in Library and Information Science, edited by Irene Owens (No. 28, 2002). *"A useful overview of marketing for LIS practitioners in a number of settings, including archives, public libraries, and LIS schools." (Barbara B. Moran, PhD, Professor, School of Information and Library Science, University of North Carolina-Chapel Hill)*

Out-of-Print and Special Collection Materials: Acquisition and Purchasing Options, edited by Judith Overmier (No. 27, 2002). *"Offers inspiration and advice to everyone who works with a special collection. Other librarians and bibliophiles who read it will come away with a new appreciation of the challenges and achievements of special collections librarians. . . . Also valuable for teachers who address these aspects of library work." (Peter Barker, PhD, Professor of the History of Science, University of Oklahoma, Norman)*

Publishing and the Law: Current Legal Issues, edited by A. Bruce Strauch (No. 26, 2001). Publishing and the Law: Current Legal Issues *provides lawyers and librarians with insight into the main areas of legal change that are having an impact on the scholarly publishing world today. This book explores constitutional issues, such as the Communications Decency Act, showing how the First Amendment makes it virtually impossible to regulate the World Wide Web. This unique book includes a history of copyright law up through current international treaties to provide an understanding of how copyright law and the electronic environment intertwine.*

Readers, Reading and Librarians, edited by Bill Katz (No. 25, 2001). *Reaffirms the enthusiasm of books and readers as libraries evolve from reading centers to information centers where librarians are now also web masters, information scientists, and media experts.*

Acquiring Online Management Reports, edited by William E. Jarvis (No. 24, 2000). *This fact-filled guide explores a broad variety of issues involving acquisitions and online management reports to keep libraries and library managers current with changing technology and, ultimately, offer patrons more information. This book provides you with discussions and suggestions on several topics, including working with vendors, developing cost-effective collection development methods to suit your library, assessing collection growth, and choosing the best electronic resources to help meet your goals.* Acquiring Online Management Reports *offers you an array of proven ideas, options, and examples that will enable your library to keep up with client demands and simplify the process of collecting, maintaining, and interpreting online reports.*

The Internet and Acquisitions: Sources and Resources for Development, edited by Mary E. Timmons (No. 23, 2000). *"For those trying to determine how the Internet could be of use to their particular library in the area of acquisitions, or for those who have already decided they should be moving in that direction . . . this volume is a good place to begin." (James Mitchell, MLS, Library Director, Bainbridge-Guilford Central School, Bainbridge, NY)*

Gifts and Exchanges: Problems, Frustrations, . . . and Triumphs, edited by Catherine Denning (No. 22, 1999). *"A complete compendium embracing all aspects of the matter in articles that are uniformly well-written by people experienced in this field." (Jonathan S. Tryon, CAL, JD, Professor, Graduate School of Library and Information Studies, University of Rhode Island)*

Periodical Acquisitions and the Internet, edited by Nancy Slight-Gibney (No. 21, 1999). *Sheds light on the emerging trends in selection, acquisition, and access to electronic journals.*

Public Library Collection Development in the Information Age, edited by Annabel K. Stephens (No. 20, 1998). *"A first-rate collection of articles . . . This is an engaging and helpful work for anyone involved in developing public library collections." (Lyn Hopper, MLn, Director, Chestatee Regional Library, Dahlonega, GA)*

Fiction Acquisition/Fiction Management: Education and Training, edited by Georgine N. Olson (No. 19, 1998). *"It is about time that attention is given to the collection in public libraries . . . it is about time that public librarians be encouraged to treat recreational reading with the same respect that is paid to informational reading . . . Thank you to Georgine Olson for putting this volume together." (Regan Robinson, MLS, Editor and Publisher, Librarian Collection Letter)*

Acquisitions and Collection Development in the Humanities, edited by Irene Owens (No. 17/18, 1997). *"Can easily become a personal reference tool." (William D. Cunningham, PhD, Retired faculty, College of Library and Information Service, University of Maryland, College Park)*

Approval Plans: Issues and Innovations, edited by John H. Sandy (No. 16, 1996). *"This book is valuable for several reasons, the primary one being that librarians in one-person libraries need to know how approval plans work before they can try one for their particular library . . . An important addition to the professional literature." (The One-Person Library)*

Current Legal Issues in Publishing, edited by A. Bruce Strauch (No. 15, 1996). *"Provides valuable access to a great deal of information about the current state of copyright thinking." (Library Association Record)*

New Automation Technology for Acquisitions and Collection Development, edited by Rosann Bazirjian (No. 13/14, 1995). *"Rosann Bazirjian has gathered together 13 current practitioners who explore technology and automation in acquisitions and collection development . . . Contains something for everyone." (Library Acquisitions: Practice and Theory)*

Management and Organization of the Acquisitions Department, edited by Twyla Racz and Rosina Tammany (No. 12, 1994). *"Brings together topics and librarians from across the country to discuss some basic challenges and changes facing our profession today." (Library Acquisitions: Practice and Theory)*

A. V. in Public and School Libraries: Selection and Policy Issues, edited by Margaret J. Hughes and Bill Katz (No. 11, 1994). *"Many points of view are brought forward for those who are creating new policy or procedural documents . . . Provide[s] firsthand experience as well as considerable background knowledge. . . ." (Australian Library Review)*

Multicultural Acquisitions, edited by Karen Parrish and Bill Katz (No. 9/10, 1993). *"A stimulating overview of the U.S. multicultural librarianship scene." (The Library Assn. Reviews)*

Popular Culture and Acquisitions, edited by Allen Ellis (No. 8, 1993). *"A provocative penetrating set of chapters on the tricky topic of popular culture acquisitions . . . A valuable guidebook." (Journal of Popular Culture)*

Published by

The Haworth Information Press®, 10 Alice Street, Binghamton, NY 13904-1580 USA

The Haworth Information Press® is an imprint of The Haworth Press, Inc., 10 Alice Street, Binghamton, NY 13904-1580 USA.

Integrating Print and Digital Resources in Library Collections has been co-published simultaneously as *The Acquisitions Librarian*™, Numbers 35/36 2006.

© 2006 by The Haworth Press, Inc. All rights reserved. No part of this work may be reproduced or utilized in any form or by any means, electronic or mechanical, including photocopying, microfilm and recording, or by any information storage and retrieval system, without permission in writing from the publisher. Printed in the United States of America.

The development, preparation, and publication of this work has been undertaken with great care. However, the publisher, employees, editors, and agents of The Haworth Press and all imprints of The Haworth Press, Inc., including The Haworth Medical Press® and Pharmaceutical Products Press®, are not responsible for any errors contained herein or for consequences that may ensue from use of materials or information contained in this work. Opinions expressed by the author(s) are not necessarily those of The Haworth Press, Inc. With regard to case studies, identities and circumstances of individuals discussed herein have been changed to protect confidentiality. Any resemblance to actual persons, living or dead, is entirely coincidental.

Cover design by Kerry E. Mack.

Library of Congress Cataloging-in-Publication Data

Integrating print and digital resources in library collections / Audrey Fenner, editor.
p. cm.
"Co-published simultaneously as The acquisitions librarian, numbers 35/36, 2006."
Includes bibliographical references and index.
ISBN-13: 978-0-7890-2833-4 (hc. : alk. paper)
ISBN-10: 0-7890-2833-6 (hc. : alk. paper)
ISBN-13: 978-0-7890-2834-1 (pbk. : alk. paper)
ISBN-10: 0-7890-2834-4 (pbk. : alk. paper)
1. Collection management (Libraries) 2. Libraries–Special collections–Electronic information resources. 3. Academic libraries–Collection development–United States–Case studies. 4. Serials librarianship–United States–Case studies. I. Fenner, Audrey. II. Acquisitions librarian.
Z687 .I58 2005
025.2'1–dc22
2004026936

Integrating
Print and Digital Resources
in Library Collections

Audrey Fenner
Editor

Integrating Print and Digital Resources in Library Collections has been co-published simultaneously as *The Acquisitions Librarian*, Numbers 35/36 2006.

The Haworth Information Press®
An Imprint of The Haworth Press, Inc.

New York • London • Victoria (AU)
www.HaworthPress.com

Indexing, Abstracting & Website/Internet Coverage

This section provides you with a list of major indexing & abstracting services and other tools for bibliographic access. That is to say, each service began covering this periodical during the year noted in the right column. Most Websites which are listed below have indicated that they will either post, disseminate, compile, archive, cite or alert their own Website users with research-based content from this work. (This list is as current as the copyright date of this publication.)

(continued)

(continued)

Special Bibliographic Notes related to special journal issues (separates) and indexing/abstracting:

- indexing/abstracting services in this list will also cover material in any "separate" that is co-published simultaneously with Haworth's special thematic journal issue or DocuSerial. Indexing/abstracting usually covers material at the article/chapter level.
- monographic co-editions are intended for either non-subscribers or libraries which intend to purchase a second copy for their circulating collections.
- monographic co-editions are reported to all jobbers/wholesalers/approval plans. The source journal is listed as the "series" to assist the prevention of duplicate purchasing in the same manner utilized for books-in-series.
- to facilitate user/access services all indexing/abstracting services are encouraged to utilize the co-indexing entry note indicated at the bottom of the first page of each article/chapter/contribution.
- this is intended to assist a library user of any reference tool (whether print, electronic, online, or CD-ROM) to locate the monographic version if the library has purchased this version but not a subscription to the source journal.
- individual articles/chapters in any Haworth publication are also available through the Haworth Document Delivery Service (HDDS).

ALL HAWORTH INFORMATION PRESS
BOOKS AND JOURNALS ARE PRINTED
ON CERTIFIED ACID-FREE PAPER

Integrating
Print and Digital Resources
in Library Collections

CONTENTS

ABOUT THE EDITOR

Audrey Fenner, MLS, BMus, BMusEd, ARCT, is Head of Acquisitions with the Congressional Research Service, Library of Congress, Washington, DC. Ms. Fenner has held professional positions in academic, research, business, government, and public libraries in the United States and Canada. She has worked in a wide variety of library settings, from a one-person branch library housed in a trailer in the Arizona desert, to the National Library of Canada, where she did cataloging and reference work in two languages. Ms. Fenner holds a Master of Library Science degree from the University of Western Ontario, London, Canada. The author of 19 published articles, chapters, and reviews, she has guest-edited three issues of *The Acquisitions Librarian* and presently edits a regular feature in *Against the Grain.*

IN MEMORIAM

Dr. William (Bill) Katz passed away on September 12, 2004. Dr. Katz was Editor of the Haworth journals *The Acquisitions Librarian* and *The Reference Librarian* as well as *Magazines for Libraries*, *RQ* (the journal of the Reference and Adult Services Division of the American Library Association), and the "Magazines" column in *Library Journal*. In addition to his contributions to library science as an author and editor, he was a much-beloved professor in the School of Information Science and Policy at the State University of New York at Albany and a mentor to many of his former students in their professional lives. His association with The Haworth Press began in 1980 and lasted more than two decades. His steady hand, friendly guidance, and steadfast leadership will be missed by all of us at *The Acquisitions Librarian*, *The Reference Librarian*, and The Haworth Press.

Introduction:
Integrating Print and Digital Resources
in Library Collections

Library collections have always included materials in many formats, and handling a mix of material types ought to be a well-documented and accepted element of library work. In recent years the scope of acquisitions has changed and the very concept of a "collection" is being redefined. Electronic resources are ubiquitous and consulting them has become routine for librarians and users. How is this situation regarded by library collection managers? Are print and digital materials truly integrated in library collections, or are they treated and maintained as separate entities?

There are difficulties in achieving a truly integrated collection, yet without integrating resources in all formats there is duplication of access, duplication of effort, and duplication of expense. Some such duplication can be seen as a necessity. For example, the bundling of print and electronic products may force librarians to purchase the same title in two formats. Restrictive licenses can prevent a public institution from providing walk-in access to the electronic version of a reference product, so the print version is also purchased and made available.

Mistaken perceptions and outmoded attitudes can play as big a part as budgetary or licensing restrictions in limiting adoption of new technical solutions and standards. The following real-life scenarios illustrate the sorts of situations that arise.

[Haworth co-indexing entry note]: "Introduction: Integrating Print and Digital Resources in Library Collections." Fenner, Audrey. Co-published simultaneously in *The Acquisitions Librarian* (The Haworth Information Press, an imprint of The Haworth Press, Inc.) No. 35/36, 2006, pp. 1-5; and: *Integrating Print and Digital Resources in Library Collections* (ed: Audrey Fenner) The Haworth Information Press, an imprint of The Haworth Press, Inc., 2006, pp. 1-5. Single or multiple copies of this article are available for a fee from The Haworth Document Delivery Service [1-800-HAWORTH, 9:00 a.m. - 5:00 p.m. (EST). E-mail address: docdelivery@haworthpress.com].

Available online at http://www.haworthpress.com/web/AL
© 2006 by The Haworth Press, Inc. All rights reserved.
Digital Object Identifier: 10.1300/J101v18n35_01

Question: Should libraries maintain archival print journal collections in some subject areas, while merely providing access in other areas? Scenarios:

- A university administrator asks that the library subscribe to a high-priced journal in print. The library has had pay-per-view access to this journal for over a year, and nobody has requested an article from it. The administrator persists in requesting a print subscription, saying that, "It may be useful in the future."
- Teaching faculty at a university insist that the library bind and retain back runs of journals rather than relying on electronic access through JSTOR. Their reason is that they want the ability to browse print volumes. Nevertheless, many bound volumes remain in pristine condition in the stacks, seldom or never touched.

Question: Do librarians distrust the stability of electronic information and its carriers? Are such suspicions used to justify continued reliance on hard copy and manual systems? Scenarios:

- The director of a small college library does not trust the acquisitions module of the library's ILS. He insists that Acquisitions staff maintain paper files duplicating all records in the automated system. As a further safeguard, he asks his secretary to enter all invoices and payments in a handwritten ledger.
- Reference librarians at an academic library worry that the ILS will "go down" frequently, depriving users of access to reference materials. For this reason, this library purchases duplicate print and online versions of indexes and other reference sources.
- A Special Collections librarian who is fearful of network "down time" insists on maintaining a card catalog for Special Collections. She refuses to allow these holdings to be included in the library's OPAC.

Question: Are library personnel being asked too frequently to accommodate themselves to change? Scenarios:

- Serials support staff at a university library send claims in personal e-mail messages to their subscription agency's customer service representative. They are reluctant to use the claiming function of the agency's Web-based customer interface.

- A long-time staff member takes early retirement rather than endure her third migration to a new integrated library system.

What focus predominates in choosing formats and technologies for a library? Is it cost? Librarians' preferences? The needs of library users? Is the decision to purchase one format over another based on the pricing model, or on the feasibility of adopting certain technologies? The articles in this volume address such questions and concerns.

ISSUES AND OPINIONS

In recent years much has been said and written about libraries and the "big deal," the purchase of access to large aggregations of materials in electronic format. David Ball argues that this type of arrangement distorts the long-standing patterns of information creation and provision among libraries, vendors and publishers. Such distortion may be detrimental to the interests of libraries and information seekers, and small publishers not included in "big deals" may be forced out of business. Ball points out that the traditional type of scholarly publishing is still preferred over alternatives because of the financial stake scholars and institutions have in established publishing processes. Consortial purchasing can continue to make hard copy attractive as a library format.

Bethany Levrault discusses the shift in emphasis from print to online resources in library reference work. Traditional principles of librarianship apply to selection of resources in all formats. Levrault considers ways that librarians can collaborate to accomplish complete integration of electronic resources into reference collections, and describes technologies and systems that can assist with this process. Levrault stresses the need to select appropriate content and make it available without regard to format, and the need to ease users' access to non-digital resources.

RESEARCH AND ANALYSIS

James Buczynski describes integrated digital and print services and collections that support instruction at Canada's largest computer studies school. Since 1999, use patterns of print and electronic IT (information technology) book collections have run contrary to all predictions and expectations. Provision of access to large e-book collections at Seneca

College has led to no decline in circulation statistics for comparable print collections.

Jay Shorten contributes a piece of investigative reporting based on ARL libraries' catalogs and home pages. Using these sources, Shorten examines practices for integrating electronic resources into the collections of ARL libraries. Are the resources available in one catalogue, multiple catalogues, or a combination of the two, depending on the type of resource?

Sarah Robbins, Cheryl McCain, and Laurie Scrivener examine the catalogs and electronic holdings lists of ARL libraries to determine if core reference titles are held in duplicate formats in library collections. The results of their study provide interesting comparisons of the treatment of resources in specific subject areas.

Kathleen Morris and Betsy Larson provide a case study of a corporate library's progression to an all-digital collection. The authors consider such topics as licensing, copyright, and new acquisitions processes and concerns. As a library acquires more electronic resources, there is clearly a need to maintain centralized information about contracts and purchases.

At the library of The University of South Carolina School of Medicine in Columbia, South Carolina, statistics on the use of print journals were kept for a ten-year period. Karen Thompson Rosati explains how these statistics, which showed a drastic decline in the use of all print serials, provided essential collection development information for selection of serials in both print and electronic formats.

HISTORIES AND PROJECTS

Several contributors to this volume have used projects in libraries where they work to focus their discussions of integrating materials in library collections. Their articles illustrate positive approaches to the problems of acquiring and providing access to resources, and managing collections.

Tracy Primich and Caroline Richardson remind us that the integrated library system is a flexible and highly developed database. It can be used and adapted to solve many problems of providing access to library materials. The writers describe how a corporate library's ILS continues to be an up-to-date tool.

Michelle Millet and Susan Mueller present one library's study of processes and workflow involved in managing paid print and electronic serials. A task force discussed such possibilities as ceasing to check in print serials, as well as the implications of proposed changes for staff workflow and user satisfaction.

Sandhya D. Srivastava and Pamela Harpel-Burke describe a serials review project in another library, involving a transition from print to online access. The authors found that, according to the literature, faculty liaisons are seldom involved in collection management decisions regarding serials. A review of Hofstra University Library's biology subscriptions shows serials evaluation in action.

Richard Jasper uses a serials cancellation project undertaken at the library of the Houston Academy of Medicine-Texas Medical Center to discuss consortial agreements for online resources in relation to collections budget cuts. Over a three-year period, the number of journal titles made available online at this library quadrupled. More than half of this increase resulted from consortial purchases.

Julia Dickinson and Sarah George of Illinois Wesleyan University tell the story of the new Ames Library building, which opened in January 2002. Initial planning called for creating a user-centered arrangement of information without regard to format of materials. While much of the collection was indeed integrated during the move to the new building, some materials remain in separate collections.

Justina Osa describes the unique problems of managing the many formats in an education library's collection. In considering educational materials, it is clear that not everything in a library can or ought to be digitized. Physical, tactile experience is very important in learning, particularly for children. Osa points out that format must never impede access to the content of library materials, and it is the responsibility of librarians to ensure that access is made simple, logical, and convenient for users.

Audrey Fenner

ISSUES AND OPINIONS

Signing Away Our Freedom:
The Implications
of Electronic Resource Licences

David Ball

SUMMARY. At first sight, the "big deal" seems an excellent value for academic libraries. A more thorough-going evaluation, however, exposes dangers. This paper examines the roles and strengths of the players in the information supply chain: creators, publishers, intermediaries, libraries. Traditional hard-copy procurement is analysed in terms of these roles and the concepts of authority, branding, and monopoly, and contrasted with the procurement of electronic resources. The advantages and dangers of the big deal are discussed. The latter arise mainly from the pub-

David Ball is University Librarian, Bournemouth University, Fern Barrow, Poole, Dorset BH12 5BB, UK (E-mail: dball@bournemouth.ac.uk).

The author is indebted to Mark Bide for his analysis of the information value chain in the 1998 study for ECUP+: *Business Models for Distribution, Archiving and Use of Electronic Information: Towards a Value Chain Perspective.*

[Haworth co-indexing entry note]: "Signing Away Our Freedom: The Implications of Electronic Resource Licences." Ball, David. Co-published simultaneously in *The Acquisitions Librarian* (The Haworth Information Press, an imprint of The Haworth Press, Inc.) No. 35/36, 2006, pp. 7-20; and: *Integrating Print and Digital Resources in Library Collections* (ed: Audrey Fenner) The Haworth Information Press, an imprint of The Haworth Press, Inc., 2006, pp. 7-20. Single or multiple copies of this article are available for a fee from The Haworth Document Delivery Service [1-800-HAWORTH, 9:00 a.m. - 5:00 p.m. (EST). E-mail address: docdelivery@haworthpress.com].

Available online at http://www.haworthpress.com/web/AL
© 2006 by The Haworth Press, Inc. All rights reserved.
Digital Object Identifier: 10.1300/J101v18n35_02

lishers' position as monopolists. Means of minimising these dangers–
consortia, alternative publishing methods, new economic models to promote competition–are examined. *[Article copies available for a fee from The
Haworth Document Delivery Service: 1-800-HAWORTH. E-mail address:
<docdelivery@haworthpress.com> Website: <http://www.HaworthPress.com>*
© 2006 by The Haworth Press, Inc. All rights reserved.]

KEYWORDS. Big deal, consortia, procurement, purchasing, electronic
resources, publishing, information chain, supply chain

INTRODUCTION

There is a common European folk-tale, often called 'the little porridge pot.' It tells the story of a family of hungry peasants who are given
a magic cooking pot by the usual mysterious outsider. They are told two
words of command: one makes the pot produce an endless supply of
porridge; the second makes it stop. The pot will obviously change the
peasants' lives: hunger, and the fear of it, will be banished by a ready,
endless supply of food: humble, monotonous perhaps in modern eyes,
but a nourishing staple. All is well; the peasants no longer go to bed hungry.

However, one day the daughter of the family is left alone in the peasants' cottage. She instructs the pot to cook; unfortunately she has forgotten the word of command to make it stop. When the rest of the family
returns that evening, the village and fields are covered in a sea of porridge, which is starting to invade the forest.

As with all folk-tales, there are many resonances for the modern
world. We live in an information-hungry society. The electronic medium, delivered through the desk-top porridge-pot, offers a means of
stilling that hunger. However the message of this paper is that, just like
the little porridge pot, electronic information is not an unalloyed good:
it has dangers and threats for the continuance of publishing and the library profession. In particular our ability to shape our collections is being eroded.

This paper discusses:

- the information value chain and some of its concepts, paying particular attention to features differentiating electronic from printed
  information;

- the implications of the product-to-service shift for archiving and access;
- business models for e-resources, particularly the big, or all-you-can-eat, deal;
- their impact on the marketplace;
- the loss of control by librarians and strategies to regain control.

The opinions expressed are my own and do not necessarily represent the views of Bournemouth University.

THE INFORMATION VALUE CHAIN

Following Mark Bide's useful taxonomy, we can identify the following activities or functions in the information supply chain: creation, publication, aggregation, access, and use. To a greater or lesser degree, each of the activities, or links, adds value to the information, until it is used and the value realised. This account is somewhat simplified: I shall not discuss exhaustively the roles of all the players in the chain, but concentrate on the key ones. Some of the main concepts applied during this discussion are: branding, authority, monopoly, and the product-to-service shift.

Each link in the chain confers an element of branding or authority on the information. Authority has to do with reliability, informed opinion, having status, or expertise. One thinks for instance of the BBC: a news broadcast in the World Service carries a great deal of authority. Branding has to do with consistency and quality. Examples might be Coca-Cola and Pepsi Cola: these are different brands, with different qualities, consistent in themselves and having different adherents.

Each link in the chain also has a greater or lesser degree of monopoly. This is obviously particularly important for the information marketplace. I shall therefore highlight where monopolies and competition lie, how they can be used to advantage, and the problems they cause the purchaser or user.

One major factor differentiating electronic from printed information is the shift from product to service. With printed information, much labour and cost are tied up in producing, distributing, storing, and handling a physical product: books and serials. With electronic information, libraries and other intermediaries generally provide only access to information held in a remote location, a service not a product. It is worth noting that this shift follows a general trend, as companies and public bodies outsource more and more activities.

CREATION

Creation is a familiar concept, and needs no great discussion. Creators may be authors or compilers. They may be directly employed by publishers, as are journalists and technical writers. Alternatively they may be independent agents.

Particularly in popular fiction, the creator confers authority. One obvious example is Stephen King: picking one of his novels from the shelf one knows what one is getting. On the cover it is his name, not the title, that has prominence. The creator is also a monopolist: only Stephen King produces his novels. This monopoly, protected by copyright, is then generally transferred to a single publisher.

PUBLICATION

Publication is essentially concerned with the selection and editing of information into consumable form. In one sense it is a form of quality control.

Publishers also package information into usable and buyable units (titles, series, journals), market the product, and undertake, or subcontract, physical production and distribution.

For librarians, authority is conferred in part at least by the imprint–Oxford University Press, for instance, or Butterworths. The end-user is more likely to focus on the brand–*British Medical Journal*, *Nature*, or *Who's Who*. This holds equally true for academic publications, where the editorial and refereeing process is concentrated at the level of the title, as for general publications.

The publisher's monopoly, often transferred from the creator, is also jealously preserved.

For those involved in procurement, the delivery of information in electronic form embodies some important differences from the delivery in printed form.

There is essentially no physical production and distribution of electronic information. There is a physical realisation at the moment of use–as an image on a computer screen or a print-out. But this occurs only at the end of the information chain, not close to the origin, as happens with print. For the rest of the chain we are talking about access to the information, not a physical product containing the information. We, as purchasers, are therefore now buying a service as opposed to a physical product.

We should also note that, with electronic information, authority is potentially diluted. It is easy to publish and disseminate information on the Web, far easier than publishing and disseminating in print, which require considerable investment of money and time. It has become correspondingly difficult to establish the authenticity and provenance of information.

AGGREGATION

One may define aggregation as: bringing together in a coherent collection disparate information sources. Clearly this is core territory for the information professional. The traditional activity of acquisition that formed our large historical libraries is now increasingly underpinned by the procurement process and the support and expertise of procurement professionals, who are bringing greater regulation and management into this process and increasing value for money for their institutions.

Libraries confer authority by virtue of selecting material. Users, whether students or members of the public, perceive a certain warranty of fitness for purpose if a book is on their library's shelves. Libraries also have a perhaps unrecognised near monopoly on such aggregations of printed information. There are few alternatives, except a bookshop, where stock, facilities, and opportunities for consultation and loan are severely limited or impossible.

It is important to note in this context the accent on the physical product. Much of a traditional library's work deals with acquiring, processing and handling these physical products. Increasingly, as far as the acquisitions process goes, this is subcontracted or outsourced to intermediaries, such as booksellers or serials agents.

With electronic information, there is no physical product to acquire or handle. The role of aggregator therefore moves elsewhere in the supply chain, to the publisher or intermediary such as the serials agent. There is also a trend to "virtual" aggregation, with services such as CrossRef, where the articles of major serials publishers are linked, while remaining on servers run by the publishers themselves.

Libraries' collective near monopoly, evident for printed information, is therefore lost: users need set foot nowhere near a library to have access to aggregators' sites; they simply need a network connection, and either the appropriate permissions or deep pockets.

ACCESS

Facilitating and controlling access to aggregated printed information is again core territory for libraries, needing little explication.

Selective dissemination of information raises awareness. Catalogues, bibliographies, and indexes aid discovery and location. User education, particularly in academic libraries, trains users in gaining efficient access to and effectively exploiting information. Library management systems control access to collections.

Libraries here, too, have a perhaps unrecognised near monopoly on providing access and the tools that support it.

Providing access to electronic information is however fundamentally different.

One prerequisite is a robust IT infrastructure to deliver the information. In the UK this infrastructure is well established in academic libraries and is becoming widespread with current investment in the public library sector.

However, many of our users have their own PCs and Internet connections. Soon set-top boxes will deliver Internet connectivity through the television screen. Provision and installation of such set-top boxes may follow the pattern established by mobile phone companies, which gave away the hardware in order to be able to sell services. Libraries therefore are fast losing the monopoly on access: the majority of our users may soon be able to connect to information resources more easily from their living rooms than from a terminal in a library.

One can also foresee existing providers of online services offering alternative public information services. The local supermarket might offer community information, added value to ensure customers return to the site for their online shopping. Why should our users move from the comfort of their homes to use our connectivity? Why, even, should they connect to, say, a public library Web site when a commercial Web site they use frequently fulfills their perceived information needs?

Libraries' collective near monopoly on providing and facilitating access to information is therefore lost. However, authority is also diluted. How far can one trust the information offered as an add-on by a commercial service-provider? For the time being libraries will retain the authority conferred by their traditional roles as selectors and organisers of information resources.

USE

Finally we arrive at the end of the chain and its reason for existence, the user, who, of course, particularly in the academic sector may also be the start of the chain.

Hitherto we have stressed that, for traditional printed resources, we have been dealing with a physical product. What we provide to the user is, however, a service–access to the information–not the physical product itself. Even in the case of photocopies, a little thought should demonstrate that this is so: the product is returned to the shelf.

Here we also have one of the conundrums of the information chain: how, particularly in the print environment, do we measure actual usage of acquired stock? We as librarians routinely collect statistics on loans, footfall, etc. But how well do these statistics reflect actual usage? Of five items borrowed, only one may be used or needed; the rest may be rejected by the borrower for whatever reason. Also, how can we effectively measure reference usage within the library, and how many libraries regularly and accurately do so?

Furthermore, if we have only a very blunt measure of usage, can we equate apparent usage with value to the end-user? If we cannot, how can we justify our purchasing decisions?

Holding information electronically offers some help here: it opens the possibility of more accurately recording and measuring usage, as expressed in access to and downloads of particular texts or services. It is also possible to envisage systems of payment for such usage, either through actual cash transactions or through users having and exchanging a number of credits. Holding information electronically therefore opens the way to more accurate measures of both usage by, and value to, the end-user.

MONEY AS AN INDICATOR OF VALUE

Let us take a little time to chart the flow of money through the value chain, and to reflect on where it sticks.

Beginning with the independent creator (i.e., one not employed to write) we note that in popular fiction the rewards tend to go to the author. Stephen King and Tolkien are commodities: their creativity is the point of scarcity, and points of scarcity tend to attract money.

Scholarly and academic authors, on the other hand, are generally paid nothing, or next-to-nothing, for their output. Scholarly journals obviously cannot exist without their output, but this dependence is not recognised in economic terms. It is the publisher, not the author, who reaps the direct financial rewards of publication. This is reflected, for instance, in the profits of the big academic publishers. Thus Houghton notes that "in 1997 Reed Elsevier enjoyed a higher net profit margin than 473 of the S&P 500 listed companies, Wolters Kluwer provided higher return on equity than 482 of the S&P 500, and margins generated in the science, technical and medical publishing areas of the companies tend to be even higher than aggregate margins" (Houghton 65).

So what are they rewarded for? Publishers in effect provide two services: firstly they disseminate information; secondly they confer authority by ensuring quality. Dissemination can be achieved by anyone with a network connection: scholars and professionals regularly use e-mail and other similar means of disseminating results. This is not therefore a point of scarcity. However, particularly with scholarly publication, publishers provide validation of results through the editorial and peer-review process. Guédon traces this process of validation, of creating the scholarly record, of establishing paternity and property rights, back to the 17th century, where it is already evident in the first issues of the *Philosophical Transactions of the Royal Society of London* (Guédon 3).

It must be remembered that scholarly and academic authors do reap indirect rewards from publication. Publication, particularly in prestigious peer-reviewed journals, leads to promotion and to research funding. There is of course institutional, as well as personal, interest, in such publication: the funding and prestige of institutions is generated in large measure by their scholars. This institutional interest is particularly evident in the UK, where the quinquennial research assessment exercise ranks university departments and disburses large sums of money to the best.

There is therefore a large financial interest, on the part of both individual scholars and their employing institutions, in continuing to play the game of scholarly publication in existing established peer-reviewed journals; this may explain, at least in part, why new electronic initiatives outside traditional publishing have not taken off.

Another interesting characteristic of the financial side of scholarly publishing is that the user or consumer in general does not pay for the information used. (Fines are levied not for the information delivered but for transgressions against an institutional code; charges for photocopies are for the convenience of the user not for the actual information.) Payment is made from an institutional budget, generally delegated to the librarian. The user is therefore insulated from considerations of cost and the effects of inflation: unlike most products, price does not affect demand because the user is not obliged to place a value on the product consumed.

THE PRODUCT-TO-SERVICE SHIFT

We have delineated a new feature of the information value chain that has important implications for collection development: the shift from buying a product to buying a service.

When we buy a physical product–a book or a journal–our users will have access to it in perpetuity. There are risks–it may be lost or vandalised or read to destruction–but we can take steps to minimise these risks. The point is that we are physical curators and in control: the right to the object is inalienable, even if there are restrictions on rights to its content. Our users know that, all things being equal, they may return to our shelves in five or ten years' time and retrieve the same item.

However, in the electronic world we do not buy and own a physical product; we buy, generally, a time-limited licence that confers certain rights of access to content. There are important differences here.

Firstly, such licences do not necessarily offer archival rights: in such cases our users do not have continuing rights of access to material beyond the term of the licence. Many of us involved in consortia take a stand against the loss of archival rights. BIBSAM in Sweden, for instance, refused in March, 2003, to continue an agreement with AAAS for access to *Science Online* in part at least because of a refusal to include archival rights. This refusal produced the interesting reaction from *Science Online* that only consortium administrators insist on archival rights; individual libraries do not. This is understandable: libraries, under immediate pressure from their users, are likely to sign agreements giving the benefits of electronic access, however imperfect; individual libraries are also quite likely to continue to purchase parallel hard copy to guarantee continuing archival access.

Secondly, the content to which we buy rights may change. Titles, imprints and companies may be bought, sold, transferred. There is a well-known example in the UK of an intermediary selling to public libraries a deal comprising access to national newspapers; all was well until the newspapers became concerned at the potential loss of revenue from CD-ROM sales and withdrew their titles. There are also well-documented examples on the e-mail lists of individual published articles being subsequently withdrawn. In short, there is no guarantee of continuing access to content.

Thirdly, licences may restrict access to content to particular classes of user. In the UK there is an increasing trend, encouraged by the government, to teaching higher education courses in colleges of further education. However licences may restrict usage to a particular site or to a particular institution, excluding students and staff elsewhere. Our freedom to determine who may have access to our resources has been forfeited.

BUSINESS MODELS

The most remarkable business model to have emerged is the so-called big, or all-you-can-eat, deal. This is particularly prevalent in the field of e-journals, but may also be seen in the field of e-books.

Under the big deal, a journal publisher will grant access to all of their titles for three or five years. There is an annual subscription, often based on the cost of the subscriber's previous print subscriptions, with some built-in increase for inflation and generally a no-cancellation clause. Libraries and their users will therefore have access to all of the publisher's content spanning however many years are available in the electronic archive.

There are potential benefits for both sides. Users have immediate access to material previously not subscribed to at no incremental cost. Libraries can predict inflation over the term of the agreement, and save money from the inter-library loans budget. Publishers have a stable revenue stream for a number of years, with no cancellations.

However, things are seldom as straightforward as they seem.

There is some statistical evidence to show that users are downloading or hitting articles well outside the range of the previously subscribed core of hard-copy titles. Understandably this has caused librarians a fair amount of anguish, since it implies that our past collecting policy has been ill advised.

However, we have to treat this evidence with some caution. It has not been collected for very long; it offers a short time series at the start of a new service. There is no real comparison with previous data: librarians have generally not collected usage data for their journals, partly because much consultation has been within the library. There is also the sweet-shop syndrome: children suddenly given the freedom of a sweet shop will gorge far beyond the value of their pocket money. The take-up of articles by academics may decline over time as the novelty disappears. Also, we may be observing the substitution of full article hits or downloads for previous use of abstracting services: because the download or consultation is free, academics may use that mechanism where they would previously have satisfied themselves with an abstract. In other words the distortion that we noted above, arising from the divorce of the user from the cost of the information, is magnified. We are perhaps even further away from measuring value to the consumer, rather than usage.

In my opinion, therefore, the prima facie case that the big deal offers major benefits in terms of access to information is not necessarily proved. Indeed there is some countervailing statistical evidence. Hamaker for instance notes that 28% of *Science Direct* titles accounted for 75% of downloads at the University of North Carolina at Charlotte. Thirty-four percent of titles had five downloads or less. Forty percent of usage occurred in a single month for 57% of titles (Hamaker 12-14). The core collection, it seems, is still alive and well.

There is also a hidden danger in the availability of the full output of some of the bigger publishers. Guédon traces the influence of the citation indexes' documentation of impact factors for journals in creating a core collection of must-have journals for particular disciplines. He also posits an increase in citations of the journals of big deal publishers (understandable given their availability) in the research output of subscribing universities (Guédon 24). We have therefore potentially a vicious circle where the journals in big deals have higher and higher impact factors, to the detriment of journals outside the big deals. The effect on the marketplace will be to undermine the financial viability of such journals and their (generally smaller) publishers.

The big deal is also challenging for librarians. Under it we no longer take the decisions on developing our collections that we have been used to (not necessarily a bad thing, some would say, given some of the statistics mentioned above). We shall increasingly decide on content not at the journal level but at the publisher level. This is a qualitative change and one that does not necessarily work in our or our users' favour. The user is focused on the article, to a lesser extent on the journal title, and most certainly not on the publisher. In the electronic environment, where the physical package–the title–is no longer necessary for purchase, our aim surely should be to increase the granularity of decision making, not decrease it.

I believe that the big deal may also presage a further unwelcome effect on the marketplace. We recall that publishers are monopolists: only they own the rights to their content and determine the terms. In the environment of consumer publications there is some substitutability: instead of buying *The Times* one can buy *The Independent*; they are different brands but with very similar news content. However, in the academic world there is virtually no substitutability of primary content. The big deal commits a library to either buy or cancel the entire content of a monopolist: the monopoly is thereby intensified. This cannot be in the interests of the purchaser. There is also a danger that, at renewal time, publishers can offer libraries a stark choice: pay an additional 50% for the big deal or cancel. Few academic libraries will be able to refuse the big deals, because they contain so many must-have titles. The consequence will therefore be that journals outside the big deals will be cancelled. Publishers, particularly the smaller ones, will cease trading, and there will be further consolidation in the marketplace.

I have dwelt here on e-journals, as the more mature electronic market. A similar characteristic is also evident in the e-books market, where some aggregators offer the equivalent of the big deal: one subscribes to all or nothing, or to business or IT libraries of several hundred titles. Again there is no selection at the individual title level, only at the library or publisher level.

It must however be said that there is also a countervailing trend in the e-book market, where at least one intermediary enables libraries to subscribe title by title and to change these titles every month.

It must be in our interests as librarians and purchasers to encourage those trends and the suppliers that offer us the flexibility and granularity that we and our users require.

WHAT CAN LIBRARIES DO?

We have seen that the marketplace is changing, that the big publishers are introducing business models that seem to benefit the user but that are potentially dangerous in their effects, threatening the viability of the smaller publishers and exacerbating the tendency to consolidation.

There are a number of measures we can take both to strengthen libraries' position and change the publishing environment.

Firstly, we can form and support library consortia. These can be powerful entities, particularly when they take a holistic view uniting both print and hard-copy procurement. They are the only library organisations that have a chance of affecting the marketplace.

Secondly, we can follow the normal procurement process. Currently we have let suppliers, the publishers, take control. We can regain it by observing the standard procurement cycle:

1. Identify the need
2. Prepare the specification
3. Find the supplier
4. Award the contract
5. Measure and monitor suppliers' performance

This cycle, particularly through the specification and by monitoring performance against that specification, puts the purchaser firmly in control. Admittedly such control is easier to achieve where there is competition between suppliers (e.g., booksellers or serials agents) and not a monopoly as with publishers. However, by allowing the publishers to dictate the terms of engagement we are ceding too much.

Thirdly, we can support alternative publishing initiatives such as SPARC. As we have discussed above, traditional hard-copy publishing in peer-reviewed journals is deeply entrenched because of institutional and personal interests in the scholarly community. These initiatives can however be held up as alternatives, even if there is little chance that in themselves they will become rivals to traditional publishing. As Guédon remarks, pitting SPARC against the big publishers is like pitting David against Goliath, but with the added disadvantage that Goliath has chosen a stone-free field of battle (16).

Fourthly, we can involve our users more. Many of the current and historical problems are exacerbated by divorcing the user from payment for information. I do not suggest that the user should be made to pay, rather that the economic consequences of their demand should be made clear to them. We can involve them more in the procurement cycle outlined above: how many consortia or individual libraries consult the end-user about the specification or include them in contract management? Furthermore, electronic publishing allows procurement decisions at a greater level of granularity–the individual article or chapter. As I have suggested elsewhere (Ball 218-220), can we not devolve such decision making to the end user rather than retaining it ourselves?

VALE

Returning to our opening folk-tale, the little porridge pot on everyone's desk is a major benefit in satisfying information hunger. However, it is vital that we, the purchasers, retain control of it by not forgetting the magic words of command, or relinquishing them to others.

AUTHOR NOTE

David Ball is University Librarian at Bournemouth University and is a leading prac-titioner in the field of library purchasing consortia. He chairs Procurement for Libraries and the Libraries Group of the Southern Universities Purchasing Consortium, and has negotiated ground-breaking agreements with suppliers for services and materials. He is a Member of the Board of the South West Museums, Libraries and Archives Council, and plays a leading role in regional library affairs in the UK. He also has experience in the private sector, as information manager for a major newspaper publisher.

REFERENCES

Ball, David. "The Information Value Chain: Emerging Models for Procuring Elec-tronic Publications." *Online Information 2000: 24th International Online Informa-tion Meeting: Proceedings.* Conference ed. Catherine Graham. Oxford: Learned Information Europe, 2000. 213-223.

Guédon, Jean-Claude. "In Oldenburg's Long Shadow: Librarians, Research Scientists, Publishers, and the Control of Scientific Publishing." *ARL Proceedings* 138 (May 2001). 7 Apr. 2003 <http://www.arl.org/arl/proceedings/138/>.

Hamaker, Chuck. "Quantity, Quality and the Role of Consortia." *ASA 2003 Confer-ence: What's the Big Deal? Journal Purchasing–Bulk Buying or Cherry Picking? Strategic Issues for Librarians, Publishers, Agents and Intermediaries. 24th & 25th February 2003, Royal College of Nursing, Cavendish Square, London.* [High Wycombe: Association of Subscription Agents, 2003.] 7 Apr. 2003 <http://www.subscription-agents.org/conference/200302/index.html>.

Houghton, John. *Economics of Scholarly Communication: A Discussion Paper Pre-pared for the Coalition for Innovation in Scholarly Communication.* Melbourne: Center for Strategic Economic Studies, Victoria University, 2000. 7 Apr. 2003 <http://www.caul.edu.au/cisc/EconomicsScholarlyCommunication.pdf>.

Integration in Academic Reference Departments: From Print to Digital Resources

Bethany R. Levrault

SUMMARY. Reference services are in the midst of evolutionary changes. At a time when budgets are shrinking, traditional models of service and print reference formats are being questioned. This article discusses future directions of academic reference collections in terms of the apparent shift from print to electronic reference sources. Questions addressed include the traditional model of reference service and how it applies to new reference formats, the extent librarians should integrate electronic resources into current collections, new technologies to assist libraries with integration, and the role of the library catalog. The author believes that although libraries need to address future technologies in order to survive as viable information providers, the core principles of the field need to play a dominant role. *[Article copies available for a fee from The Haworth Document Delivery Service: 1-800-HAWORTH. E-mail address: <docdelivery@haworthpress.com> Website: <http://www.HaworthPress.com> © 2006 by The Haworth Press, Inc. All rights reserved.]*

KEYWORDS. Academic libraries, values, integration, electronic resources, hybrid libraries, cataloging

Bethany R. Levrault is Reference Librarian, Regina Library, Rivier College, 420 Main Street, Nashua, NH 03060 (E-mail: blevrault@rivier.edu).

[Haworth co-indexing entry note]: "Integration in Academic Reference Departments: From Print to Digital Resources." Levrault, Bethany R. Co-published simultaneously in *The Acquisitions Librarian* (The Haworth Information Press, an imprint of The Haworth Press, Inc.) No. 35/36, 2006, pp. 21-36; and: *Integrating Print and Digital Resources in Library Collections* (ed: Audrey Fenner) The Haworth Information Press, an imprint of The Haworth Press, Inc., 2006, pp. 21-36. Single or multiple copies of this article are available for a fee from The Haworth Document Delivery Service [1-800-HAWORTH, 9:00 a.m. - 5:00 p.m. (EST). E-mail address: docdelivery@haworthpress.com].

Available online at http://www.haworthpress.com/web/AL
© 2006 by The Haworth Press, Inc. All rights reserved.

Digital Object Identifier: 10.1300/J101v18n35_03

No matter what species you are examining, environmental changes will drive evolution of that species. As we proceed into the twenty-first century, academic reference services continue to be in the midst of their own evolution, often at remarkable speeds. Shrinking budgets, smaller numbers of staff, and the proliferation of electronic databases and Web resources are just a few of these changes. It is no secret that the academic library is in the midst of a "technological revolution," where "digitization, networking and information" [. . .] are "sweeping across the globe and exerting great influence upon social, political, economic and cultural activities as well as people's daily lives" (Lu 14). In the reference department, librarians face their own set of challenges, such as the extra time needed to learn new electronic databases, the stress of meeting the heightened demands of patrons, and often, the confusion in determining the core functions of the job itself (Reger 73).

The pace of this change has raised troubling issues for the reference profession. Just what is the role of traditional academic reference services in the 21st century? And what types of materials will comprise the typical reference collection in thirty years? Will patrons continue to use items in paper format, or will e-books and electronic collections continue to be a patron's primary sources? In the 1990s, the typical library was primarily concerned with print collections, preservation, and development of automated cataloging systems (Saunders 2). Today, many libraries have achieved automation of tasks once done manually but are facing larger, more tumultuous issues.

At the crux of these issues is the integration of electronic resources and existing materials, many of them still in traditional print format. Librarians continue to struggle over what print resources to update and which to cancel entirely. This decision is not always an obvious one. The library as it has traditionally existed in an academic institution is facing an uncertain future. For example, Billings suggests that the academic library of 2013 will operate on transformational changes that are "wild card" (105) in nature.

Not only are libraries lacking sufficient models demonstrating how to maintain the cost of new digital materials (Oder S74), they are also increasingly trying to "do more with less." As a library becomes increasingly scaled back, librarians are questioning their fundamental values (Honan). For example, library administrators hesitate to spend thousands of dollars on a resource that will be outdated or be vastly underutilized in a couple of years. The fact that a librarian working fifty years ago in an academic library probably would not even recognize many of the tasks of the typical reference or cataloging librarian of to-day (Helfer 39) makes the questions even more unsettling. Patrons who increasingly "expect to get everything they need fulltext and immedi-ately and are frequently disappointed by anything less" (41) are not an exception, but the norm. In addition, concern over preservation of digi-tal media, an increasing problem (Warner 47), has caused us to wonder about our roles as collectors and instead think of ourselves as ac-cess-providers.

If provision of access, rather than storage and preservation, comprise the primary functions of the reference department, additional questions can be raised about what model should be utilized. Libraries increas-ingly exist in "an ambidextrous universe–equally print and electronic" (Wilkinson and Lewis 15), and the implications of this existing hybrid are ambiguous. Should e-books be cataloged alongside traditional print materials, or should they exist in a separate database? Should Web sites be selected and cataloged, when one has only to type a few short keywords into a search engine and retrieve thousands of pages of re-sults? Will Generation Y embrace printed materials as a reference source, or do they consider them a waste of time? Such questions are just the tip of the iceberg.

In response to these changes, this article will discuss future directions of academic reference collections in terms of the obvious shift from print to electronic reference sources. Questions to be addressed include the extent to which traditional principles of librarianship apply to cur-rent resources, the extent to which libraries should integrate electronic resources into current collections and with whom and how the library should collaborate to accomplish integration, new technologies avail-able to assist in integration, and the role of the library catalog. Many scenarios are possible for the academic reference department of the fu-ture.

THE CONTAINER vs. THE CONTENT

When speculating on the future of the reference collection, it is easy to let technology dominate the discussion. Descriptions of recent hy-brids such as London Public Library's "Idea Store" (Lane) and Emory University's "Information Commons" have forced us to think about the impending direction of our own libraries and how technology will play a voluminous role. Articles that frequently appear in daily newspapers, such as a recent *New York Times* article entitled "Online Library Wants It All, Every Book" (Worth), despite its cautionary tales of technical and logistical obstacles to digitizing every available book, nevertheless assumes that this will eventually take place. Similarly, the apparent blurring of many academic libraries into mini information technology departments, where students regularly request help with Microsoft Office products and courseware modules such as Blackboard or WebCT, make many wonder where the library in its traditional form fits into our technologically-oriented world. What are our values? And what should they be?

It is now "almost a platitude to state that the traditional paradigm of librarianship is rapidly changing" (Nisonger 639). However, a paradigm is different from a principle. Although the methods of access to information may have changed, the principles of the profession–connecting the user to the information she or he needs–are the same as they have been for decades (Curry 1). People will still need help with their research no matter what the format of the information. Technology will not change that basic principle. As librarians, we need to keep these principles in mind when regularly confronted with situations that illustrate the problems with technology, such as a database devoid of information on a patron's topic, or a Web site whose authority is questionable. Despite technology's advances, patrons still seem to acknowledge these principles; most seem to know that a librarian is a person who helps them find information, no matter what the format.

Even if we acknowledge that as reference librarians our primary function is to help people find information, additional questions can still be raised. If technology will be the primary "container" for information instead of a library shelf, then one might suppose that many library functions could be taken over by the information technology department. Many librarians assume that information technologists could never take over the functions of an academic library. However, information technologists are proficient with information organization and presentation, just like librarians. Database vendors often hire people without any formal library training. But potential does not equal reality. As librarians, we are much better suited to take advantage of selecting, organizing, and preserving digital information (Warner 49) just as we have done with information in all other type of formats. Simply stating that others could do our jobs does not mean that they will.

WALKING A DELICATE LINE

Applying this same basic principle of librarianship–connecting the user with the information sought–suggests that we should continue to evaluate new electronic resources in terms of benefit to our users. Who are our users? What do they want? If a business sees their customer base declining, that business would try to determine "what it is not doing right" (Tennant 2) and modify its practices accordingly. This same evaluation applies to libraries. By looking at a new resource, database, or Web site in terms of where it fits into the existing collection and whether or not it would be of benefit to the library's users, librarians will not be led astray into trying to predict the future or the next "hottest" trend–and potentially, into wasting thousands of dollars. It is better to approach evaluation of reference resources using the same principles that reference librarians have used for those in traditional formats (Whitlatch 21) than to put all our faith into one technology or format that ultimately proves to lack value.

In light of traditional goals, we might take a simpler approach when faced with an impending budget deadline and multitudes of offerings from vendors. An approach where "the library's service goals and the appropriate roles technology plays in supporting these goals" (Penka 1) maintains that delicate balance between traditional structures and new technologies. Balance is the key–each new database, approach, or vendor should be implemented in moderation lest the vendor file for bankruptcy in a few years.

Even more importantly, we should not sell ourselves short when regarding the skills we have. This can be hard to resist, particularly when we are around the technologically-inclined. But we must. As Sara Weissman states, "You may not know JavaBeans, but you do know what is and what is not authoritative information" (44). It is easy to forget that so much of reference work comes down to basic human intelligence which cannot be easily duplicated by any type of technology, relevance algorithm, script, or artificial intelligence system. By using our acquired skills to evaluate technology in terms of where it fits into the existing library structure without placing blind faith in it, we acknowledge technology's tremendous importance without investing indiscriminately in the next hottest database or trend. The best approach to take involves linking new technology with traditional library services, keeping in mind that we have a job to do no matter how we do it–helping people find information.

INTEGRATION AND ACCESS

If librarians acknowledge that the best approach resolves around users, then we must acknowledge change. In the current environment, no library will succeed "without incorporating technology into daily operations" (Thomas 1). The way we search for and access information is changing almost daily–certainly monthly–and many of the resources once considered useful for years are now out of date in months. The shorter shelf life of a resource is even more pronounced in the science and technology collections. Technology integration changes "what and how much librarians can do" (Tenopir), so librarians must acknowledge and be responsive to these changes.

In response to the changing landscape, most libraries are transitioning to an environment that is rich in technology in an effort to provide the latest information at the fastest pace (Murgai 6). But how can we integrate access to material to establish "bibliographic control," as it were, over all these different formats?

The answer, ironically, will probably be found in technology, with networking and the Web taking the obvious role. We know that electronic information is pervasive in the lives of our users, particularly those of younger generations. It is common knowledge that "more and more students are going first to the Web to meet their information needs; many go no further" (Marcum 2). A 2002 user survey at Rivier College's library in Nashua, New Hampshire shows this trend. When asked the question, "If you have not used the library within the past year, please state why," one student answered, "I normally just go onto the Internet and get my information there" ("2002 User Survey Results," 3). Many more undoubtedly will do the same.

As a result of the Web's ubiquitous influence, particularly as a starting point for research, many students will simply ignore the materials available in other formats, even if those materials are more suitable for a particular assignment. Since students often ignore sources not immediately available to them via a computer screen, it makes sense to try to achieve true integration of all materials in all formats. How else will students realize that resources exist if these resources have not been integrated into one interface? Good librarians "are aware of and value the whole world of recorded knowledge and information–from books, maps, videos, electronic resources, and everything in between" (Gorman 4). We need to make sure the typical user does, too. By providing seamless access via a Web browser to information in all formats, we make sure our users recognize–if not value–print formats as well.

THE PATH OF LEAST RESISTANCE

In some ways, arguing for integration is simply arguing for proximity. Librarians have long known that placing similar resources in close proximity increases circulation and user access. Electronic activity stimulates use of print material (Mason 15). Even simply placing books en route to a library's computer lab may increase use of these books drastically (Bratton). This is not surprising, since people will use whatever methods are most convenient. Applying this idea to the lack of consciousness of print resources, Tennant calls this "the convenience catastrophe," which is nothing more or less "than the disappearance of our print collections in the face of more easily obtained digital content." Following this line of reasoning, if we provide access to material in all formats via our online catalogs, then we are well on our way to creating a virtual space where all types of material can easily be identified, in the same way as we have already created bricks-and-mortar library space.

Providing information about material in all formats brings us one step closer to insuring that students are using authoritative information rather than a Web site of questionable authority. Tennant makes a similar point when he says, "How do we fight this tendency [over-reliance on the Web]? We must provide more information online about what our print collections hold, so that potential users of our holdings can more easily discover the treasures they contain." Other authors agree with this hypothesis: "Without these [electronic] resources, students will use their own devices to locate information on the internet. Not only is this approach more difficult, requiring them to do the sifting of Web sites, but they are far more apt to use non-relevant, low-quality, and even erroneous information in their research" (Weisberg and Toor 2). Like the esoteric object hidden in the back of the second-hand store, students may come to view books in the same way–separate–and less useful than the other big-ticket items being sold. If we do not provide integration, we may be forgoing access. The path of least resistance will then hopefully lead a student to the best resources available, regardless of format.

TOOLS FOR INTEGRATION

User surveys undertaken at many institutions support the idea of resource integration. A 2002 survey of students, undertaken at the University of Oklahoma, called for several changes in their academic library, including staff training, development programs, and better "integration of traditional [print] and electronic resources" (Hahn 18). A UCLA library survey conducted in the same year stated a similar need, showing that patrons demanded "integrated access to resources beyond the library's print holdings of books and journals, especially links to electronic books, journals, and databases" ("Orion2 Replacement"). A similar proposal currently under consideration at Macon State calls for the library to "integrate current library technology with the continued development of traditional print sources" ("Library for the 21st Century"). An integrated system with material in all formats displayed in one interface prevents confusion on the part of users and eliminates the need to check through multiple areas for information.

Although supported by survey data, integration is not an easy goal. Academic librarians face many challenges when trying to implement integration, not the least of which is the tremendous amount of time needed to evaluate new products and determine which information will be of value given their current collection (Brooks 316). Checking lists of journal titles contained within a database being considered for purchase against the current collection, for example, is not a quick and painless task. Coverage of each resource may be spotty, and some vendors operate on a rolling coverage schedule, where issues are added at the expense of elimination of older issues. Additionally, a confusing myriad of products, services, and new technologies now exist for resource integration. Most likely, weaving all the sections into one seamless entity will be achieved using a combination of these resources, differing among libraries according to user skills, information needed, and budgetary constraints. It is a daunting task.

New technologies from vendors provide one answer. Many are now offering several different products to help solve the integration issue. The NetLibrary Reference Center is just one such example of the integration that is increasingly becoming important to librarians and patrons alike. Instead of laboriously scanning through indexes and table-of-contents pages, NetLibrary has combined the full text of several popular reference titles into e-book format, the texts of which can all be searched at the same time, using one search box. This functionality, although lacking somewhat in the full-text searching arena (users can search only by subject headings), takes much less time for the user and is decidedly more comprehensive, an obvious advantage. NetLibrary's popularity continues to grow; as of 2003, about 8,000 libraries currently used NetLibrary's products and services (Lorenzo). The Gale Literature Resource Center provides a similar structure, combining into one interface author biographies, literary criticism, and additional resources.

Libraries can expect the popularity of electronic access to continue. Instead of scanning indexes, library users will continue to prefer to type subject words into a search box to search all the library's reference books simultaneously in electronic format. However, at least for the foreseeable future, tools of this nature are probably only part of the equation. Although promising, they are too new for us to judge whether they will completely surpass print. The next few years suggest that a hybrid model, where both print and electronic collections will exist together, will be the most prevalent.

THE HYBRID LIBRARY

As we have discussed, users want seamless access to materials in all formats. However, many of our primary reference works are still in traditional formats. This presents a problem both for access and for organization.

The model that is most probable for libraries, at least for the next few years, will likely continue in the form of a "hybrid library." A hybrid library is a library "where 'new' electronic information resources and 'traditional' hardcopy resources co-exist and are brought together in an integrated information service, accessed via electronic gateways available both on-site, like a traditional library, and remotely via the Internet or local computer networks" (Hutton). This term seems to have originated in Europe (Schwartz 385), but applies to libraries in all countries. Of primary importance to the hybrid library is that of seamless access to resources regardless of format. In practice, this type of library would probably provide a unified interface, where users could type in search terms that would then search the entire world of available contents of any particular library, whether print or electronic. The easiest analogy is that of a Web meta-search that would redistribute a query into multiple engines and return results from all resources on one integrated screen.

Maintaining a hybrid library is not an easy task. It will require visionary leaders who are able to think "outside the box," and to establish multi-skilled teams of information specialists collaborating together to deliver the service (Von Elm and Trump 34). A related type of library is the digital library, a collection of digital works that are linked together by an underlying unified structure and that serve a specific user community or set of communities (Schwartz 385). Whether any particular library stays in hybrid form or transcends to a digital structure will depend on the library. No matter what the model, librarians will need to be flexible and innovative to keep pace with these technologies while keeping them in line with the library's vision (Von Elm and Trump 33).

Vendors are also using technology to provide seamless access to resources. EBSCO, for example, provides linking services from one database to another, so that fulltext from any one EBSCO database a library subscribes to can be accessed from any other database. Frequently, such as is the case with The Gale Group ("Gale Adopts"), this type of technology involves use of the SFX OpenURL standard, a technology that links databases to one another at the document level no matter their source. The goal of SFX is to present information to the user in a standardized interface which takes into account the context of the entire collection that is available (Van de Sompel and Hochstenbach 3). This standardized interface makes finding information, at least in theory, easier than it has ever been for a library user. Ex Libris's recent announcement of the availability of Books24x7 content in both its MetaLib and SFX products ("MetaLib and SFX") demonstrates the rapid addition of content to these systems.

REFERENCE LIBRARIANS AND EDUCATORS

Integration is happening at the department level as well as the resource level. The Library of Congress's Global Reference Network, a "collective of libraries and librarians formed to provide professional input on issues such as digital reference 'Best Practices' and policies" ("Global Reference Network") attempts to provide both librarians and patrons with the professional expertise of others in the field. Networking of this type is nothing new, and probably has been common among librarians since the profession's inception. However, by formalizing it as a service within itself, it is just another step toward the integration of all available information resources, regardless of place, person, or format. Through the Global Reference Network's QuestionPoint service, library patrons have the ability to submit questions at any time of the day or night through their own library's network. An answer is then provided by either a librarian in their own library or by another librarian anywhere on the network.

Unlike integration of resources using SFX-type systems, this type of integration is probably the least likely to happen on any large scale. Although patrons are demanding integration of all resources within their local library, and a need and desire clearly are evident from user surveys, reference collaboration of this sort is probably unnecessary. Reference librarians are fielding fewer questions, not more, and usually are successful answering questions using locally accessible resources. As Coffman states, collaborative digital reference such as QuestionPoint is simply a "solution without a problem" (57). Further, statistics suggest that collaborative digital reference services are failing before they even have a chance to get off the ground–witness the Collaborative Digital Reference Service's statistics of only about 2,000 questions referred to the system within the first two years of its use (58) even though over 260 large libraries were participating. Two thousand might appear to be a substantial number; however, this averages to only seven questions per library over a two year period.

Integration sometimes means the actual merging of the library and the IT department into an "Information Commons," mentioned earlier. This is the case at Bucknell University, Carthage College, Connecticut College, and Wheaton College, and is under consideration at schools such as Carleton College, Columbus State, and Illinois Wesleyan (Schulz). Merging the academic library with the IT department may work for many schools, and if it does happen, it raises additional questions of roles and responsibilities among staff.

Libraries and academic departments often work together as well. A recent article that appeared in *The Chronicle of Higher Education* describes two such institutions where faculty members and librarians are slowly, but surely, starting to work together on courseware (Carlson). Libraries have always collaborated with academic departments through liaison work, but not always in building technology. With library resources maintained as part of course Web sites, rather than separately, the probability of students using library databases and journal articles has increased, and the "fight against Googling" (Carlson) has slowly begun.

STANDARDS–OR LACK THEREOF

When integration is discussed, one of the largest issues is the direction and future of the library catalog. If we need to provide access to resources anytime, anywhere, then the catalog, or some incarnation of it, is the obvious choice for connectivity.

Use of the library catalog as a means to organize electronic resources alongside traditional ones is not as easy as it might seem. MARC records and library catalogs are poorly suited to providing integrated access to all the electronic content now available (Scharf 21). Since ISBD was developed for printed materials, it tends to be very good at describing these types of materials and not so good at describing online sources. For example, a book always has an author, a title, and publication date, but a Web site may not always have the same data elements. Issues of catalog format are being addressed somewhat by value-added additions to catalog records such as the MARC 856 field ("Guidelines for the Use of Field 856"), and by documents that describe how to catalog online resources, such as Nancy B. Olsen's "Cataloging Internet Resources." The Library of Congress's Network Development and MARC Standards Office has developed a schema for a bibliographic element set called the Metadata Object Description Schema which is a set of standards, using XML code, which enables the cataloger "to carry selected data from existing MARC 21 records as well as to enable the creation of original resource description records" ("Metadata Object Description Schema"). Using resources such as MODS, traditional library catalogs can be modified to take digital resources into account.

An additional group working on similar issues is the Dublin Core Metadata Initiative, the mission of which is "to make it easier to find resources using the Internet" ("The Dublin Core Metadata Initiative"). Work on developing metadata standards for Internet resources has been adopted by seven countries and is under discussion in several more. Similarly, Z39.50 standards have made it easier for us to search several different library catalogs at once (Dowd). Development of these standards is both needed and important, but it will take some time for these multiple initiatives to form cohesive structures that are workable.

The future of the library catalog and the directions of cataloging internet resources are beyond the scope of this paper, but it is obvious that whatever forms the catalog takes, integration of multiple formats will have to be taken into account. Existing catalog structures will eventually be enhanced depending on needs. One thing is clear—today's online reference sources are evolving into creatures very different from their printed ancestors (Winter 72). And in any process of evolution, ineffective models become extinct species. Let's not let the academic library become one of them.

SELECTED RESOURCES

Chandler, Yvonne J. "Reference in Library and Information Science Education." *Library Trends* 50 (2001). Library Literature, WilsonWeb. Simmons College Lib. 26 Feb. 2003 <http://hwwilsonweb.com>.

Dowd, John. "Digital, Virtual–Dream or Reality? Building the Electronic Library: The OCLC Experience." 19 Mar. 2003 <http://www.iatul.org/conference/fullpaper/dowd.html>.

"Gale Adopts SFX Open URL Standard." *E-Content News* (2001). 29 Mar. 2003 <http://www.econtentmag.com/r10/2001/ecnews12dd.html>.

"Gale–Literature Resource Center." *Thomson Gale.* 29 Apr. 2003 <http://www.galegroup.com/LitRC/>.

"Guidelines for the Use of Field 856." *Library of Congress.* 20 Mar. 2003 <http://www.loc.gov/marc/856guide.html>.

Hoyer, Rüdiger. "Electronic Art Reference." *66th IFLA Council and General Conference*, Jerusalem, Israel, 13-18 August 2000. 7 Mar. 2003 <http://www.ifla.org/IV/ifla66/papers/076-109e.htm>.

"Information Commons Home." *Emory University.* 19 Mar. 2003 <http://infocommons.emory.edu/>.

Jones, Chris. "Development Strategies for Library Collections in a Digital Environment." *Australasian Public Libraries and Information Services* 14 (2001), 101-107. Library Literature, WilsonWeb. Simmons College Lib. 20 Mar. 2003 <http://hwwilsonweb.com>.

Lane, Megan. "Is This the Library of the Future?" *BBC News World Edition* 18 Mar. 2003. 19 Mar. 2003 <http://news.bbc.co.uk/1/hi/uk/2859845.stm>.

"MetaLib and SFX from Ex Libris to Provide Access to Books24×7 On-Line Referenceware–Integration Brings Wider Search Capabilities to Academic Libraries through Powerful Unified Interface." *Ex Libris.* 25 Mar. 2003 <http://www.exlibris-usa.com/news1.asp?categoryId=155&admin>.

Miller, Ruth H. "Electronic Resources and Academic Libraries, 1980-2000: A Historical Perspective." *Library Trends* 48 (2000): 645-670.

"NetLibrary Reference Center–New Product Information." *NetLibrary.* 29 Apr. 2003 <http://www.netlibrary.com/help/reference_center.asp>.

Olsen, Nancy B. "Cataloging Internet Resources: A Manual and Practical Guide." 20 Mar. 2003 <http://www.purl.org/oclc/cataloging-internet>.

Singh, Neena. "Internet: Importance and Usage for Library and Information Professionals." *DESIDOC Bulletin of Information Technology* 21 (2001): 17-28. Library Literature, WilsonWeb. Simmons College Lib. 13 Mar. 2003 <http://hwwilsonweb.com>.

REFERENCES

"2002 User Survey Results." *Rivier College.* 2002. 18 Mar. 2003 <http://www.rivier.edu/support_services/regina_library/default.asp?id=57>.

Billings, Harold. "The Wild-Card Academic Library in 2013." *College & Research Libraries* 64 (2003): 105-109.

Bratton, Phyllis Ann K. E-mail to the College Libraries section of ACRL. 26 Mar. 2003.

Brooks, Sam. "Integration of Information Resources and Collection Development Strategy." *The Journal of Academic Librarianship* 27 (2001): 319-319.

Carlson, Scott. "New Allies in the Fight Against Research by Googling." *The Chronicle of Higher Education* 49 (2003). 19 Mar 2003 <http://chronicle.com/free/v49/i28/28a03301.htm>.

Coffman, Steve. "What's Wrong with Collaborative Digital Reference?" *American Libraries* 33 (2002): 56-58.

Curry, Evelyn L. "Technological Advances in Reference: A Paradigm Shift?" *Library Trends* 50 (2001). Library Literature, WilsonWeb. Simmons College Lib. 26 Feb. 2003 <http://hwwilsonweb.com>.

"The Dublin Core Metadata Initiative Overview." *DCMI.* 23 Mar. 2003 <http://dublincore.org/about/overview/>.

"Global Reference Network." *Library of Congress.* 20 Mar. 2003 <http://www.loc.gov/rr/digiref/>.

Gorman, Michael. "Values for Human-to-Human Reference." *Library Trends* 50 (2001). Library Literature, WilsonWeb. Simmons College Lib. 26 Feb. 2003 <http://hwwilsonweb.com>.

Hahn, Susan E. "Assessing Customer Demands: Making Changes That Count." *Library Administration and Management* 16 (2002): 16-23. Library Literature, WilsonWeb. Simmons College Lib. 18 Mar. 2003 <http://hwwilsonweb.com>.

Helfer, Doris Small. "Back to the Future: A Look at the Past to Get a Glimpse of the Future." *Searcher* 10 (2002): 38-41. Library Literature, WilsonWeb. Simmons College Lib. 20 Mar. 2003 <http://hwwilsonweb.com>.

Honan, Jim. "How Do We Become Tomorrow's Leaders: Librarians Positioning for the Future." *ACRL New England Conference: Libraries & Librarians: Positioning for the Future* (24 Mar. 2003).

Hutton, Angelina. "The Hybrid Library." 7 Mar. 2003 <http://hylife.unn.ac.uk/toolkit/The_hybrid_library.html>.

"Library for the 21st Century." *Macon State College.* 2001. 19 Mar. 2003 <http://www.maconstate.edu/library/century_library.html>.

Lorenzo, George. "NetLibrary's EBooks a Growing Phenomenon." *Educational Pathways* 15 (Mar. 2003). 19 Mar. 2003 <http://www.edpath.com/netlibrary.htm>.

Lu, Ji. "Creating Special Literature Resource Databases in Western China Under a Digital Environment." *Bulletin of the American Society for Information Science and Technology* 29 (2003): 14-19. 12 Mar. 2003 <http://www.asis.org/Bulletin/Feb-03/ASISTFebMar.pdf>.

Marcum, Deanna B. "Realizing the Potential of Digital Libraries." *CLIR Issues* 32 (2003). 14 Mar. 2003 <http://www.clir.org/pubs/issues/issues32.html>.

Mason, Marilyn. "Cleveland Public Redefines Patron Usage in Electronic Age." *Library Journal* 123 (1998): 14-15. Library Literature, WilsonWeb. Simmons College Lib. 20 Mar. 2003 <http://hwwilsonweb.com>.

Murgai, Sarla R. "When Library Surveys Result in Positive Action: A Success Story." *Tennessee Librarian* 53 (2002):5-23. Library Literature, WilsonWeb. Simmons College Lib. 20 Mar. 2003 <http://hwwilsonweb.com>.

Nisonger, Thomas E. "Introduction, Collection Development in an Electronic Environment." *Library Trends* 48, 639-644. Library Literature, WilsonWeb. Simmons College Lib. 20 Mar. 2003 <http://hwwilsonweb.com>.

Oder, Norman. "Online Resources Emerge." *Library Journal, Supplement* 121 (1996): S74-S76.

"Orion2 Replacement User Survey Report." *U of California at Los Angeles Lib.* 2002. 18 Mar. 2003 <http://www.library.ucla.edu/otng/survey_report.html>.

Penka, Jeffrey T. "The Technological Challenges of Digital Reference." *D-Lib Magazine* 9 (2003). 14 Mar. 2003 <http://www.dlib.org/dlib/february03/penka/02penka.html>.

Reger, Nancy K. "Redefining Reference Services: Transitioning at One Public Library." *Reference & User Services Quarterly* 38 (1999): 73-75. Academic Search Premier, EBSCOhost. Regina Lib. 9 Mar. 2003 <http://search.epnet.com>.

Saunders, Laverna M., and Maurice Mitchell. "The Evolving Virtual Library: An Overview." *The Evolving Virtual Library: Visions and Case Studies*. Ed. Laverna M. Saunders. Medford, NJ: Information Today, 1996. 1-17.

Scharf, Davida. "XML Under the Hood." *Information Outlook* 6 (2002): 20-27.

Schulz, Kathleen M. "Summary of Information Commons." E-mail to the College Libraries section of ACRL. 24 Mar. 2003.

Schwartz, Candy. "Digital Libraries: An Overview." *The Journal of Academic Librarianship* 26 (2000): 385-393.

Tennant, Roy. "Digital Libraries: The Convenience Catastrophe." *Library Journal* 15 Dec. 2001. 29 Mar. 2003 <http://libraryjournal.reviewsnews.com/index.asp?layout=article&articleid=CA185367&publication=libraryjournal>.

Tenopir, Carol. "Electronic Reference in Academic Libraries in the 1990s." *Annual Review of OCLC Research* 7 Mar. 1995. 7 Mar. 2003 <http://www.oclc.org/research/publications/arr/1995/part4/sect4.htm>.

Thomas, Mary Augusta. "Redefining Library Space: Managing the Coexistence of Books, Computers, and Readers." *The Journal of Academic Librarianship* 26 (2000): 408-415.

Van de Sompel, Herbert and Patrick Hochstenbach. "Reference Linking in a Hybrid Library Environment. Part 2: SFX, A Generic Linking Solution." *D-Lib* 5 (1999). 7 Mar. 2003 <http://www.dlib.org/dlib/april99/van_de_sompel-pt2.html>.

Von Elm, Catherine and Judith F. Trump. "Maintaining the Mission in the Hybrid Library." *The Journal of Academic Librarianship* 27 (2001): 33-35. Library Literature, WilsonWeb. Simmons College Lib. 20 Mar. 2003 <http://hwwilsonweb.com>.

Warner, Dorothy. "'Why Do We Need to Keep This in Print? It's on the Web . . .' A Review of Electronic Archiving Issues and Problems." *Progressive Librarian* 19/20 (2002): 47-64. Library Literature, WilsonWeb. Simmons College Lib. 20 Mar. 2003 <http://hwwilsonweb.com>.

Weisburg, Hilda K., and Ruth Toor. "The E-Reference Collection." *The School Librarian's Workshop* 23 (2002): 1-2. Library Literature, WilsonWeb. Simmons College Lib. 20 Mar. 2003 <http://hwwilsonweb.com>.

Weissman, Sara. "Shoptalk: Answers to Real-World Problems." *Library Journal* 125 (2000) 44, Academic Search Premier, EBSCOhost. Regina Lib. 9 Mar. 2003 <http://search.epnet.com>.

Whitlatch, Jo Bell. "Evaluating Reference Services in the Electronic Age." *Reference & User Services Quarterly* 38 (1999): 73-75, Academic Search Premier, EBSCOhost. Regina Lib. 9 Mar. 2003 <http://search.epnet.com>.

Wilkinson, Frances C. and Linda K. Lewis. "Reference Materials–Stalking the Wild Electron: Librarians and Publishers Speak Out!" *Against the Grain* 12 (2000): 15-16, 18, 20, 22.

Winter, Ken. "From Wood Pulp to the Web: The Online Evolution." *American Libraries* 31 (2000): 70-74.

Worth, Robert F. "Online Library Wants It All, Every Book." *New York Times on the Web* 1 Mar. 2003. 25 Mar. 2003 < http://www.nytimes.com/2003/03/01/arts/01ALEX.html>.

RESEARCH AND ANALYSIS

Debunking
the Computer Science Digital Library:
Lessons Learned
in Collection Development
at Seneca College
of Applied Arts & Technology

James Andrew Buczynski

SUMMARY. Developing a library collection to support the curriculum of Canada's largest computer studies school has debunked many myths about collecting computer science and technology information resources. Computer science students are among the heaviest print

James Andrew Buczynski is Information Services Librarian, Seneca College of Applied Arts & Technology, Learning Commons, Seneca @ York Campus, 70 The Pond Road, Toronto, Ontario, Canada M3J 3M6 (E-mail: james.buczynski@senecac.on.ca).

[Haworth co-indexing entry note]: "Debunking the Computer Science Digital Library: Lessons Learned in Collection Development at Seneca College of Applied Arts & Technology." Buczynski, James Andrew. Co-published simultaneously in *The Acquisitions Librarian* (The Haworth Information Press, an imprint of The Haworth Press, Inc.) No. 35/36, 2006, pp. 37-53; and: *Integrating Print and Digital Resources in Library Collections* (ed: Audrey Fenner) The Haworth Information Press, an imprint of The Haworth Press, Inc., 2006, pp. 37-53. Single or multiple copies of this article are available for a fee from The Haworth Document Delivery Service [1-800-HAWORTH, 9:00 a.m. - 5:00 p.m. (EST). E-mail address: docdelivery@haworthpress.com].

Available online at http://www.haworthpress.com/web/AL
© 2006 by The Haworth Press, Inc. All rights reserved.
Digital Object Identifier: 10.1300/J101v18n35_04

book and e-book users in the library. Circulation statistics indicate that the demand for print format books is not declining in relation to the rapid development of digital library collections. The digital library is evolving alongside the traditional physical library and the funding implications of building two collections are substantial. E-book demand is skyrocketing as collaborative online learning takes hold in community colleges. *[Article copies available for a fee from The Haworth Document Delivery Service: 1-800-HAWORTH. E-mail address: <docdelivery@haworthpress.com> Website: <http://www.HaworthPress.com> © 2006 by The Haworth Press, Inc. All rights reserved.]*

KEYWORDS. E-books, budgets, computer science, technology training, digital libraries, community college libraries, textbooks, publishing industry

Today's generation of students is the first to grow up surrounded by digital media and communications. "For the first time in history, children are more comfortable, knowledgeable and literate than their parents about an innovation central to society" (Tapscott 1). Computer science and computer technology education programs are prospering on a combination of this enthusiasm for using computer technology and the insatiable demand of industry for highly skilled graduates. Seneca College of Applied Arts & Technology is both Canada's largest community college and computer studies school. Developing a library collection to meet the swelling demand for computer technology information resources has debunked many myths about collecting to support computer science curricula.

Computer science students are heavy book users, contrary to popular belief. The administrative dream of the computer science digital library is a far cry from the reality of patron demand. The demand for print format books is not declining in relation to the increasing availability of electronic books (e-books). Students are demanding the development of digital library collections alongside traditional print collections and the funding repercussions are troubling. News reports concentrating on the demise of e-book publishing hide the fact that computer technology e-book publishing is booming. Custom e-book textbooks are already appearing in the marketplace. "There is a shift away from the pedagogy, art, science and profession of teaching to the creation of learning partnerships and learning cultures" (Tapscott 148). As collaboration moves into an online environment, library collections are evolving to support these new learning communities.

CANADA'S LARGEST APPLIED TECHNOLOGY COLLEGE

Seneca College of Applied Arts & Technology, located in Toronto, Canada, is Canada's largest community college, with more than 16,000 full-time and 90,000 part-time students spread across nine campuses. The college offers more than 230 diploma programs and four Bachelor's degree programs. The School of Computer Studies at Seneca, with more than 2,600 full-time students, is the largest computer studies program in Canada and graduates more than 20% of all computer studies diploma students in Ontario. The program specializations include: Computer Programming and Analysis, Object-Oriented Programming, Internet Systems Administration using Linux, Computer Networking and Technical Support, Computer Systems Technologist, and Bachelor of Applied Technology Software Development. In addition to the computer science programs the college offers state-of-the-art programs in 3D animation, business information systems, digital media arts, digital media technical production, graphic design, Web content development, and Web programming.

More than 90% of the print collection and the administration of electronic resources that support the computer science and digital media curricula at Seneca are located in the Learning Commons at the Seneca @ York campus. The campus is located on the grounds of York University and comprises a state-of-the-art Technology Enhanced Learning (TEL) building that is shared with York University. The Learning Commons facility is comprised of a large computer lab with 300 computer workstations (one of many labs on campus), inviting quiet study lounges, a library, and a learning/tutoring center. The reference and computer laboratory assistance services are integrated at a single service point. The desk is staffed at all times by both library and IT staff. The Help Desk handles everything from research questions to College e-mail, courseware, and server access to programming assistance. Network ports for students with laptops are also available in public areas and student lounges. Several computer technology programs are located on other campuses which do not have physical libraries.

PRINT COLLECTION

The Seneca @ York campus library collection began in 1998. Collection profiles were developed for each College school and can be seen on the College Web site. Print materials were acquired, guided by these plans. The collection development vision aimed to build a critical collection size over a five-year period. Today, the Computer Science and Digital Media Arts collection has attained the desired holdings size, and looking back, several lessons were learned. The lessons learned were twofold: the demand for print monographs is not declining in relation to the increasing availability of e-books, and e-books increase demand for print books as well as additional e-book titles. The late 1990s administration dream of the college library with declining physical holdings is not coming to fruition. Furthermore, the myth of computer science monograph obsolescence has been exposed through user demand for dated titles. The digital library has grown up alongside the traditional library and the result is collection development costs and shelving requirements beyond our wildest imaginations five years ago.

The sheer number of students and computer science classes offered at Seneca @ York have been continually growing over time. The circulation stress this demand places on our collection is astounding. The mass appeal of many computer science areas related to the World Wide Web compounds this problem. Specifically, students taking classes in disciplines other than Computer Science or Digital Media Arts seek out many of the same practical how-to titles used by Computer Studies students. The books are used for self-study, whether it is creating a Web page, adding programming to a Web site, or configuring a Web server. Furthermore, College faculty and staff also use the collection to get quickly up to speed on a new technology, application, or programming language they have yet to encounter. Each budget year, numerous titles were acquired to both cover each specialized topic taught at Seneca and maintain up-to-date information resources for the rapidly evolving computer technology used at Seneca and by business and industry.

COURSE TEXTBOOKS

One key lesson learned was misreading the demand for college course textbooks. To have even a small percentage of thousands of students looking for course textbooks and improvising using the general circulating collection is a recipe for chaos and dissatisfaction with library service. Keep in mind that the information being sought is practical "how-to" information as opposed to specialized subject treatment in other disciplines. Monograph substitution is easily applied. A policy of acquiring one copy of each course textbook was instituted. The idea was to provide "some" access to monographs used as course textbooks. The access was in no means meant to replace the purchasing of textbooks and the restricted "two hour reserve" access assigned to the titles makes using the library's copy as a textbook for the whole course, by many students, impractical. As a side effect, the older editions of course texts are kept in the collection and can be circulated. The addition of access to large computer technology focused e-book collections unintentially assisted in balancing the demand and supply for course books and will be explored further on. The important point to note is that when both an online edition and a print edition are available, demand for the print edition remains substantial in spite of its accessibility limitations.

MYTH OF OBSOLESCENCE

There are two prevailing myths about computer science and digital media arts monographs: first, students in these curricula are the most digital information literate of all students and prefer online information over print information; and second, computer technology books become obsolete quicker than any other discipline's monographs. In both cases, there is an obsolescence myth. If the students do not demand print books, the belief is that it is only a matter of time before publishers scale back in selling them and libraries stop collecting them (Lynch 2). The myth that they go out of date very fast provides justification for librarians to stop collecting them and in their place, acquire access to e-book collections such as Books24×7 and Safari Tech Books Online.

The discipline that can achieve the "digital library" first, is believed to be computer science. In practice, this is not the case. To begin with, Seneca @ York's collection of monographs older than two or three years continues to circulate even though newer more relevant material is available. It is not uncommon for students to pull 5 to 7 books on SQL, UNIX, or database design, scan the content, and choose the one book that is either laid out to match their learning style or contains the "how-to" information they seek. In many cases it is not the most recent book on the topic. Old software support books for desktop applications also continue to circulate because students often do not have the latest applications on their home computer. A book on Office 97 is exactly what they may be seeking. Clearly, weeding is still necessary, and perhaps the collection only needs one or two monographs covering a specific version of a dated application, rather than 10 or 15. Keep in mind that the goal of the college library is to adequately support the curriculum research of students, not necessarily to provide a comprehensive repository of scholarly knowledge. The implication, however, is that Seneca @ York's shelf space requirements are greater than originally allocated in 1999 and the library part of the Learning Commons facility was expanded in mid-2003 to address this reality. The demand for print books continues to be healthy which makes the "Digital Only Library" further away than faculty thought back in 1999.

E-BOOKS

Through experience, our predictions of the consequences of acquiring computer technology e-books have proven false. First a definition of e-books is necessary to clear up any misconceptions:

> A digital book is just a large structured collection of bits that can be transported on CD-ROM or other storage media or delivered over a network connection, and which is designated to be viewed on some combination of hardware and software ranging from dumb terminals to web browsing on personal computers to the new book reading appliances. (Lynch 4)

The hype surrounding e-books is based largely on their inherent advantages over print format books:

- Accessible anytime, anywhere, especially from courseware Web sites.
- Eliminates the need for duplicate copies across campuses.
- Enables multiple simultaneous user use.
- Fully searchable across a specific title or across multiple titles. Hit lists range from page level to chapter level access.
- Fully browse-able online.
- Computer code examples can be "cut-and-pasted" into programming editors.
- Linked directly to dictionaries, for word look-up.
- Do not become damaged or lost.
- Titles are often available online prior to print availability.
- Content can be updated/corrected after initial publishing.
- Books can be annotated/book marked without damaging the book.
- There are no processing fees for overdue items.
- Few acquisitions labor processing costs.
- No real estate consumption.

E-book vendors over the last few years have marketed their products to academic libraries as a cheaper more accessible collection of "how-to" computer technology books, than traditional print collections. We bought in to the idea that in the near future we could drastically scale back our acquisitions of print format computer technology books and through e-book collections meet the information needs of our users better than we ever had in the past. We could offer more with less expenditure on processing labor, purchase costs, space requirements, and circulation labor.

SENECA COLLEGE'S COMPUTER TECHNOLOGY E-BOOK COLLECTION

Seneca College subscribes to three large e-book collections: Books24×7, Safari Tech Books Online, and NetLibrary. Chart 1 below summarizes the attributes, pricing, and accessibility of each collection.

CHART 1. Comparison of E-Book Collections

	Books24×7	Safari Tech Books Online	NetLibrary
Service 1st Offered	2,000	Summer 2002	1999
Number of Titles Available	2,000+	600+	50,000+
Number of Publishers Included	70+	10+	N/A
Book–Companion CDs*	No	No	No
Built-In Dictionary	No	No	Yes
Book Page Format	Web	Web	Web
Acquired Access	Spring 2002	January 2003	Summer 2002
Consortium Package	No	No	Yes
Number of Titles Available at Seneca College	2,000+	100	500+ Computer Science Titles**
Number of Simultaneous Users	Unlimited	10	1 user per title
Pricing	Site Licence	Tokens (Bundles of titles)	Consortium Collection (Retail + Access fee)
MARC Records	Yes	Forthcoming	Yes
Patron Profile and Login Required	No	No	Yes
Search Across Books	Yes	Yes	Yes
Browse Subject Trees	Yes	No	No
Lists Recently Added Books	Yes	N/A	N/A
Lists Forthcoming Books	Yes	N/A	N/A
Search Programming Code Fragments	No	Yes	No

* Electronic editions of books generally do not include access to "Companion CDs" included with Print editions.
** 500 Computer Science Titles within the Consortium of Ontario Libraries collection of 6,500+ titles.

Books24×7

Books24×7 is both the largest (number of titles and diversity of publishers) and most heavily used e-book collection at Seneca College. The size of the computer technology title collection dwarfs the other two collections and the unlimited simultaneous user licence is a hit with students. There are no "turn-aways." At the beginning of our subscription, Seneca had a limited number simultaneous user licence. After a promotion campaign to faculty and students and the addition to our library catalogue of MARC records for each title in the collection, usage exploded. "Turn-aways" became a huge problem. An unlimited user licence was purchased in the Fall 2002 semester. Other notable aspects of the Books24×7 service are the ability to search for titles by browsing subject term hierarchies and the ability to access the service without first having to create a "User Login Profile." Students seek instant access and in today's Login/Password overloaded world, spending two minutes to create a login and password (they often forget the ones they create) is an exercise in frustration. Netlibrary requires users to create a user profile, to use a title for an extended period of time (online check-out), and students regularly express their dislike of this digital rights management system.

Safari Tech Books Online (ProQuest)

Safari Tech Books Online was acquired in January 2003 to provide access to publishers no longer available in the Books24×7 collection. The absence of online access to new O'Reilly titles was a significant gap in our e-book collection. The print titles are heavily used by students. One hundred key titles were selected from a list of more than 600 titles. Pricing is based on the token model, which Safari calls "bookshelf slots." Bundles of bookshelf slots with limited simultaneous user levels are purchased and titles are selected to fill these analogous bookshelf slots. Most titles use one slot; however, some use less and certain titles use more. Titles can be added by purchasing additional bundles or by weeding the online collection. Titles can easily be dropped after 30 days and replaced with new acquisitions. This practice is discouraged, however, since each addition and deletion of a title generates cataloging work. Besides the exclusive content available from the service, the ability to search for programming code fragments is valued by students. This search functionality is unique to Safari. Students experiencing programming problems, especially syntax errors, can type in a code fragment and search for similar examples across all the books in the collection. For example, this C++ programming code fragment: "std::ostream&, const Array&" can be searched. This searching capability is far from refined and some trial and error is required. Overall the code fragment search is a great feature that Books24×7 lacks.

NetLibrary (OCLC)

Approximately 500 of the 7000 titles in Seneca's Consortium of Ontario Libraries (COOL) NetLibrary e-book collection are computer technology titles. The bulk of the collection provides e-book content for other subject areas, especially business. Although this is the case, 13 of the top 20 titles accessed in Fall 2002, were computer technology titles. Although students have a strong preference for the Books24×7 platform, largely due to the breadth and depth of the collection, as well as familiarity, they are willing to use whatever service the information is hosted on, including Safari and NetLibrary. Listing all of the titles in the NetLibrary collection in the library catalogue is key for channeling students to NetLibrary. Without the MARC records, most students would "stick with what works," namely Books24×7, instead of exploring the other e-book collections. Over 65 languages are spoken on campus on a daily basis and so it is not surprising to see students sitting in front of computers with pocket translators or print dictionaries. NetLibrary provides a built-in dictionary on its e-book platform, a helpful tool for our many ESL (English as a Second Language) students.

CIRCULATION STATISTICS REFUTE OUR PREDICTION

Circulation statistics for computer science print format monographs, however, have not crashed. Three patterns have emerged: circulation statistics for print books have fallen less than 5%, acquisition requests for specific titles have increased, and our total acquisitions budget for computer technology monographs has more than doubled.

Comparing the circulation statistics of Fall Semester 2001 with Fall 2002 reveals a decline of less than 5%. Inter-campus loans for computer science and computer technology monographs have fallen more than 60%. This figure is not shocking since few students will take the time to fill out an inter-campus loan request form, if the title sought or a similar one is available online. Seneca's history of inter-library loan requests of computer technology titles is so statistically low, the impact of e-books on these statistics was not analyzed.

Examining only the circulation of print books does not reveal the whole picture. The circulation statistics for both print and online combined have increased exponentially. Although e-book vendor-supplied access statistics are generally not aggregated in any meaningful way, what is clear from browsing the unaggregated data and anecdotal evidence from faculty, students, and vendor representatives is that the computer technology e-book collections are being accessed at a higher rate than any other online resource the library subscribes to. Certain online e-book titles are being accessed hundreds of times per week. In any case, few recently published, online titles are accessed only once per week, matching our circulation period for print books. The vendor imagineered prediction of crashing circulation statistics for print computer technology "how-to" books has generally not come to fruition except in the area of inter-campus loans. The demand for campus copies of books held at other campuses has declined thus reducing the need for duplicate copies of titles across campuses.

STUDENTS USE E-BOOK COLLECTIONS AS A BOOKS-IN-PRINT CATALOGUE

One advantage to performing collection development on a medium-sized college campus is that collection development can in practice be very demand driven. Communication between all front-line staff across numerous service desks and collection development-responsible front-line staff is relatively seamless due to the small size of the team. Demand for specific titles, publishers or subject areas is quickly relayed to collection development staff for further investigation of demand. Since acquiring access to computer technology e-books, the patron demand for specific book titles has increased. The e-book collections to some extent are being used as a shopping catalogue. Students routinely search the library catalogue for a print edition of a book they have been using online. The reasons for this will be covered later. If not held in the library, they are beginning to ask either why the library does not hold it or request that we acquire a print edition for the library. A knowledge base is used to track gaps in our collection and if numerous requests are made for a specific title or subject area the decision is made to acquire a print edition of the book title in question or acquire books in the specialized area where the collection is weak.

THE FLOODGATES ARE OPEN

The overall track record of e-book publishing is not good. The much publicized initial bankruptcy of NetLibrary, EarthWeb's discontinuation of its popular ITKnowledge e-book service, and the continuing struggles of Questia suggest e-books are floundering and either may not ever gain acceptance or the publishing model continues to be years away. E-books overall may be struggling but e-books in certain subject areas are booming. Computer science and technology e-books have gained rapid acceptance for several reasons. First, the most significant factor undermining e-book acceptance today is the usability of current computer display technologies. Reading long texts online over long periods of time is very hard on the eyes. "How-to" computer technology books however, are not read linearly or sequentially. These monographs are accessed by rapidly scanning indices and table of contents, and then going directly to the chapter or page providing the information sought. The online readability dilemma affecting other types of e-books is minimized by this pattern of usage.

Searching capability is key when using computer technology books. Online e-book collections can be searched more rapidly and effectively than print collections. This functionality steers students to e-book collections even if they seek a print book to meet their information needs. Searching the library catalogue, at best, provides searching capability down to the chapter title. This ability is the exception rather than the norm in our library catalogue. Online e-book collection searching provides full-text searching and a hit list at the chapter or page level across all the books in the e-book collection. Clearly, as a finding aid, e-book collections are a valuable source of information for students. If a print edition is sought, the student can search the Library Catalogue with a list of desired titles in hand.

NEW LEARNING COMMUNITIES

E-books are accessible to our computer technology students, wherever they are, at their time of need. Computer technology homework is very time consuming and information barriers are frequent. Knowledge base roadblocks pop up regularly. "Why isn't it working?" and "How do I do this?" are common types of problems. Students are expected to work through these barriers both to develop their knowledge base and to gain mastery of the technology being studied. In practice this means turning to friends, consulting published information sources, and talking with computer lab supervisors and tutors. Besides interacting face-to-face in labs on campus, today's students work in an online "chat" communication environment. The dubious "Chat" window is always open for synchronous text communication. E-mail is used as a document sharing-medium through "file attachment." E-mail is also used for asynchronous online collaboration, when interaction is necessary but schedules are not in synch. E-book information is easy to share in these virtual study groups. Answering someone's technical question by saying "I got the answer in this book I have signed out from the library" does not help the student in time of need. They need the answer now, to continue to the next hurdle. Similarly, it is easier to point to the answer in an e-book collection than write out the ten steps the answer requires. E-books enable online peer support and assistance that print books cannot provide. Print books are limited to individual study in today's learning environment.

DEMAND FOR E-BOOKS IS GROWING

The demand for e-book collections is developing as existing subscribed e-book collections become the key information source for students. O'Reilly publishes some of the most sought after computer science textbooks. O'Reilly decided early on in the development of the e-book publishing paradigm, that they would stop "giving away" their content to the big computer technology e-book distributors and vendors (O'Reilly, "Ecology"). Safari Tech Books Online, a partnership between Proquest and O'Reilly, is the exclusive vendor for O'Reilly e-books. Since demand for the print editions of O'Reilly titles is very high it is not surprising that students would demand online access to these titles. Although the pricing schema for Safari was far from attractive compared to our other e-book vendors, the decision was made to subscribe based on student demand for online access.

FUNDING TWO LIBRARY COLLECTIONS

Library collection development budgets are increasingly being taxed by the demand dichotomy for print and digital collections. This is especially problematic for books. Anecdotal evidence suggests that student preference for e-journals over other formats is enabling libraries to discontinue print and microform format serials subscriptions. Unable to afford collecting in both formats, electronic format, the format of choice by library users, is being selected. As a result library collections are rapidly migrating to electronic-only serials collections, whenever available and economically viable. The initial duplication of journal formats is ending, resulting in substantial savings. Digital Rights Management Systems (DRMS) for e-books however, are undermining the acceptance of e-books as a substitute to print format books. Given the eye-strain limitations of extended online reading, students seek to print chapters of books just as they do with e-journal articles. E-book DRMS's bar sequential printing and, thus, are dividing demand between print and e-books.

A Digital Rights Management System is software that enforces control over intellectual property, such as limiting downloading, printing, and copying. Publishers are relying on inconvenience, lack of cost effectiveness, and users' respect for copyright law and intellectual property to constrain copying by individuals (Lynch 16). E-book collection vendors generally limit the extent of content viewable at one time to one page. This limitation, not applied to e-journal collections, frustrates and aggravates users of e-book collections. Attempting to save or print several consecutive pages of a specific e-book either one at a time or by using Web spiders, robots or browser download accelerators (NetJet, NetSonic, MSIE Crawler, Teleport Pro), results in the user being ejected from the service. Repeated attempts in a short period of time result in the service being blocked to all users of Seneca College for a short indeterminate time.

Publishers are using technology and new legal frameworks to create new revenue opportunities while striving to maintain existing publishing revenues (Lynch 16). Publishers hope to direct a percentage of e-book users to purchase a print copy of the e-book being used. This e-book collection as "shopping catalogue" concept was explored earlier. Limiting downloading and saving also addresses the fear of runaway illegal dissemination of their property on file sharing networks. Book publishers do not want to suffer the fate of the music industry with MP3s on file sharing networks. The impact on libraries is a demand for book-based technical information in two formats, at increased cost. As long as current DRMSs remain in place, the likelihood of migrating to electronic format books and drastically decreasing print book purchases is low. This duplication of formats fiscal reality is a problem when collection development budgets are stagnant or declining and users are demanding increased access to content in the digital libraries academic institutions are building.

DISAGGREGATING THREATS

The cost of providing access to computer technology e-book collections represents almost forty percent of Seneca College's total computer technology book budget. The trend towards disaggregation is resulting in: increased subscription costs to identical content, increased administrative management costs, and decreased accessibility. O'Reilly began the march towards disaggregation by refusing to partner with the computer technology e-book vendor ITKnowledge. Most e-book vendors give publishers a percentage of subscription revenue as a royalty. The royalties are generally low. In the case of ITKnowledge, the royalty to all participating publishers was to split 20% of the revenue from subscriptions. For O'Reilly, this calculated to 15% of the 20% paid out as royalties. This minuscule amount forced them to decline the offer to partner (O'Reilly, "Ecology"). Furthermore, O'Reilly did not want to be bundled with their competitors. They partnered with the Pearson Technology Group and ProQuest to develop Safari Tech Books Online. The royalties paid to publishers are more attractive, however, the subscription costs for libraries are also substantially higher than the "Big Deal" of 2000+ titles offered by Books24×7. The Books24×7 subscription costs per title are a fraction of those under Safari's pricing scheme.

Since the debut of Safari Tech Books Online, several publishers have ceased supplying titles to Books24×7 and are partnering with Safari Tech Books Online instead. Safari is gaining the exclusive access to new titles released. In terms of maintaining access to published content, this represents a substantial increase in subscription costs. To maintain access to these publishers libraries must pay more than they did when the publishers were accessible from Books24×7. For Seneca College students, unless funding for collections increases to match these mounting subscription costs, either the number of titles accessible online will decline or cuts will be made to the print collection development budget. In any case, the trend will stress the collection development budget.

Acquiring e-books title by title and maintaining the currency of these collections is more labor intensive than subscribing to "Big Deal" collections that continue to grow in size and coverage over time. The selection of titles, verification of access title by title, MARC record loading and weeding of these e-book collections adds to the workload of already overburdened library collections development and cataloging staff.

Safari Tech Books Online has a pricing system based on tokens ("bookshelf slots"). Bundles of tokens are purchased, with limited simultaneous user levels. Titles can be dropped after one month and new titles added to replace the weeded titles without incurring an increase in costs. Additional tokens can also be acquired on a regular basis to build the collection without dropping titles. Unless libraries pressure publishers to use "Big Deal" aggregators like Books24×7, more and more publishers will migrate to the more costly "token" subscription model thereby reducing the number of e-book titles available to students.

The evolution of e-journal publishing from a few vendors and products to today's information universe of thousands of products and hundreds of vendors suggests e-book publishing will follow a similar path. Students searching for information today must choose from as little as a few dozen to hundreds of online services accessible through their institution's library. The sheer number of options has reduced accessibility to information for novice searchers. As the number of e-book services accessible through the library increase, the searching accessibility declines. Anecdotal evidence suggests that college students use a satisficing decision model for research. They locate a few relevant titles and then stop looking. On a broader level, they search only as many information services as needed to find a few titles. The more services there are available, the higher the likelihood that they will not search all the e-book collections available to find the best sources to meet their information needs. The introduction of Safari Tech Books Online, for example, has not drawn much use because students more often than not find what they are looking for in the larger and more familiar Books24×7.

Disaggregation access limitations can be mitigated by adding the MARC records of e-book titles to your library catalog. Librarians have learned over the past few years how labor intensive catalog maintenance can be for e-journals. Many have turned to third party solutions such as Serials Solutions because they cannot keep up with title additions and deletions. It is easy to imagine e-book access requiring similar solutions in the near future. Disaggregation will fuel demand for third party solutions to e-book access problems. Although acquiring subscription access to e-book collections is relatively easy the technical services ramifications stand to grow in complexity.

CONCLUSION

The digital library myth affects computer science and computer technology collection development more than any other discipline. The misconception that computer studies students "don't need books" is refuted by stable circulation statistics for computer technology books in print format and exploding online circulation transactions. In the future, more detailed analysis of e-book access statistics needs to be performed to understand better the patterns of e-book access by Seneca's students and faculty. The statistics provided by e-book vendors are difficult to interpret because of the lack of a clear and consistent definition of data elements. Computer technology students, however, are clearly the heaviest users of Seneca's York campus book collections.

E-books offer both simultaneous access possibilities that are impossible with the physical editions of books and the opportunity for online peer collaborative learning. Large low cost e-book collection vendors are facing disaggregation threats as primary publishers partner with more expensive, limited simultaneous user, title-by-title e-book disseminators such as NetLibrary and Safari Tech Books Online. The ability to maintain simultaneously growing print and digital collections is in jeopardy.

The continuing maturity of the e-book publishing industry is creating exciting opportunities for collection development. NetLibrary's e-book collection recently surpassed 50,000 titles and many of the gains have been from science and technology publishers. The time has come to revisit the development of our NetLibrary collection to address technology areas not covered by our existing e-book collections. Kluwer's e-book service is offering custom e-books (Adobe E-book Reader® formatted) based on the chapter level content of their book catalogue. Purchasers select chapters, create a personalized title and a table of contents is generated. The custom e-book is delivered in print or electronic format. Acquiring customized e-textbooks for online course reserve collections may not be too far off.

Digital rights management systems combined with the limitations of computer display technologies are undermining student acceptance of electronic only access to book based information. If the dream of the digital library is to be fulfilled these e-book problems must be addressed. Until then the computer science and technology digital library remains a distant point on the horizon.

REFERENCES

Lynch, Clifford. "The Battle to Define the Future of the Book in the Digital World." *First Monday* 28 May 2001. 12 Mar. 2003 <http://www.firstmonday.dk/issues/issue6_6/lynch/index.html>.

Nawotka, Edward. "Questia.com Slashes Staff to Save Cash." *Publishers Weekly* 248.48 (2001). Wilson Web. Library Literature and Information Full Text. Seneca College Lib., Toronto, ON. 12 Mar. 2003 < http://wilsontxt.hwwilson.com/pdfhtml/01035/1Z8YL/RS7.htm>.

O'Reilly, Tim. "Ecology of E-Book Publishing." *Digital Rights Management and Digital Distribution for Publishing, San Francisco, 15-16 August 2000*. Transcript. 12 Mar. 2003 <http://tim.oreilly.com/publishing/drmtalk.html>.

Tapscott, Don. *Growing Up Digital: The Rise of the Net Generation*. Toronto: McGraw-Hill, 1998.

What Do Libraries Really Do with Electronic Resources? The Practice in 2003

Jay Shorten

SUMMARY. One hundred fourteen academic libraries in the United States and Canada are surveyed for the organization of electronic resources within their home page and their cataloguing practice. The majority provide access to databases, electronic resources, subject guides, ready reference, and their own catalogue both on their home page and within their Web site. They usually provide links to electronic resources in the catalogue, though the practice is consistent neither among each other nor within themselves. *[Article copies available for a fee from The Haworth Document Delivery Service: 1-800-HAWORTH. E-mail address: <docdelivery@haworthpress.com> Website: <http://www.HaworthPress.com> © 2006 by The Haworth Press, Inc. All rights reserved.]*

KEYWORDS. Academic libraries, electronic resources, home page, Web site, organization, cataloguing

Jay Shorten is Cataloguer, Monographs and Electronic Resources, Bizzell Library, University of Oklahoma, Norman, OK 73019 (E-mail: jshorten@ou.edu).

[Haworth co-indexing entry note]: "What Do Libraries Really Do with Electronic Resources? The Practice in 2003." Shorten, Jay. Co-published simultaneously in *The Acquisitions Librarian* (The Haworth Information Press, an imprint of The Haworth Press, Inc.) No. 35/36, 2006, pp. 55-73; and: *Integrating Print and Digital Resources in Library Collections* (ed: Audrey Fenner) The Haworth Information Press, an imprint of The Haworth Press, Inc., 2006, pp. 55-73. Single or multiple copies of this article are available for a fee from The Haworth Document Delivery Service [1-800-HAWORTH, 9:00 a.m. - 5:00 p.m. (EST). E-mail address: docdelivery@haworthpress.com].

Available online at http://www.haworthpress.com/web/AL
© 2006 by The Haworth Press, Inc. All rights reserved.

Digital Object Identifier: 10.1300/J101v18n35_05

INTRODUCTION

How do libraries organize their electronic resources? Although no one has prescribed a standard way of doing it, has one developed anyway from librarians' daily practice? Have cataloguers solved the vexing one- vs. two-record approach to electronic resources, even though AACR2 is silent about the matter?

One can only answer such questions for the current moment. What may be the standard today can be changed tomorrow. Though practices may be evanescent, nevertheless it is still useful to investigate them, both for the theoretical reason that knowing the current practice will help theoreticians to improve it, and for the practical reason that knowing the current practice will save librarians time in deciding what to with electronic resources, whether they decide it is something to do or not to do.

LITERATURE REVIEW

Surveys of libraries' practice with electronic resources are not so common as theoretical works on Web resources, reports on how individual libraries have organized their Web pages, or papers on how to design Web resources.

John J. Riemer (1999) surveyed 62 CONSER libraries' cataloguing practices for electronic serials subscribed to within aggregator databases and found 60% made a list of e-journal titles on their Web site, 65% used one record for both print and electronic and 42% used separate records.

Linda A. Rich and Julie L. Rabine (1999) examined 114 academic library Web sites in 1997 for the types of electronic journals (free or restricted-access), the arrangement of titles (alphabetical title lists were the most popular), the accessibility of the e-journal page, the presence, location, and informational content of annotations (76% had annotations, most of them on the same page as the e-journal list) and other features, such as links to other parts of the Web page. They repeated (2001) the survey with the same libraries in 2000 and found the trends had continued upon the same lines: alphabetical title lists were even more popular and 83% had annotations that offered more information more frequently. They added an investigation of the libraries' cataloguing practices for e-journals: of the five journals they searched for, 33% of libraries catalogued all five and 96% catalogued at least one.

They also (1999) compared research university and two-year college library Web sites in 1998 for their Web sites' use as an informational, reference, research, and instructional tool and measured the sites' complexity. In that study, 100% of research universities and 84% of two-year colleges had their own catalogue (or catalogues), 88%/66% linked to other catalogues, 84%/60% linked to Net resources, and 98%/72% linked to databases.

Hal P. Kirkwood (2000) examined the Web sites of 63 academic business libraries' business collections for their types of materials and their organization in 1999. Eighty-four percent had Web catalogues, 83% vendor databases, and 95% Web resources, and the most common method of organization (87%) was to arrange their resources in groups by subject matter.

Abdus Sattar Chaudhry and Makeswary Periasamy (2001) examined 19 libraries' cataloguing practice for e-journals: 21% used the single record approach, 26% used separate records, and 53% used both.

Nestor L. Osorio (2001) examined 45 science and engineering library Web sites in 2000 for the pages' design elements (such as links, colours, images, fonts), the types of links, both to resources and to information about the library on the home page (of 47 types of links, 76% of libraries had links to the catalogue, 67% to electronic databases, 60% to full-text journals, 38% to electronic resources, and 38% to Internet resources), the number of entry points, the link to the catalogue (of one electronic journal searched, 89% of libraries had it in their catalogue and 76% had a hyperlink to it within the catalogue), and the distance in clicks to the different resources (usually between two and three).

Julie M. Still (2001) examined 150 academic libraries in Australia, Canada, the U.K., and the U.S. for their Web pages' elements and resources. All libraries had their own catalogue somewhere in the page, 100% in Canada and 92% in the U.S. had links to other catalogues, 92% in Canada and 90% in the U.S. had encyclopaedias, all libraries had databases, 84% in Canada and 92% in the U.S. had reference links, and 68% in Canada and 92% in the U.S. had Internet subject resources.

HOW DO LIBRARIES ARRANGE THEIR ELECTRONIC RESOURCES?

During February 2003, the Web pages of the 114 Association of Research Libraries (ARL) academic libraries were examined in order to find:

1. To what types of electronic resources did they typically provide access? and;
2. Do they have any common practices of arranging their electronic resources?

The ARL libraries were chosen because as academic libraries and research libraries, they would be more likely to provide many types of electronic resources to their patrons and therefore have more need to organize them than a public or community college library would. However, one would also expect them to have similar types of electronic resources, for one would expect the basic electronic resource needs of scholarly researchers to be similar.

From the full list of ARL libraries, the subset of non-academic institutions that belonged to ARL was discarded (such as the Library of Congress) as they were either too specialized or would be expected to have a different clientele; in short, they would likely have different types of electronic resources and so not be comparable to the academic libraries. This left a population of 114 academic libraries.[1]

Each library's home page was viewed with Internet Explorer 6.0 and examined for their links to electronic resources. Three libraries' home pages consisted of a list of their branch libraries. For these three, the home page of the main library was examined. Some libraries had links to a proposed new version of the Web page; these new versions were ignored. The libraries' Web pages were simply described and their characteristics were noted. No attempt was made to criticize their design on such aspects as whether they were simple to use, whether they were organized appropriately, whether they lacked easy access to certain resources, or whether they were aesthetically pleasing.

Basic Organization of Home Pages

The home page is especially important as it provides a look at what a library considers important enough or in high enough demand to provide convenient, almost instant, access. Links to electronic resources can be either present or absent on the library's home page, even if the library owns them. For example, one library may provide a link to electronic journals directly from the home page while another may require the user to go to a subsidiary page first. Each link may either have a separate existence on its own with no relation to any other link, or be grouped together with other links.

The links to electronic resources on the home pages (and only those providing access to electronic resources, whether directly or indirectly) were thus examined to see if the usual practice was to give them independent existences, or whether they were gathered together in larger groups. Some electronic resources had links in both manners on the same page: for example, a library may provide access to databases under both an "electronic resources" category and with a separate "databases" link elsewhere on the page. In such a case, the link was counted as if it had an independent existence alone. Some libraries had links on the home page to different arrangements of electronic resources, such as a link to the databases arranged by subject and a link to the databases arranged alphabetically. In this case, as the links were to the same type of electronic resource it was counted only once.

No libraries in the 114 completely lacked links on their home pages. All libraries had at least one link to an electronic resource (or to a page of electronic resources), even if it was only to the catalogue.

A minority of libraries (33, 29%) had only independent links to their electronic resources. Most libraries (78, 68%) grouped together their links in two levels, while a very few (3, 3%) grouped their links in three levels. No library used more than three.

Tables 1, 2, 3, and 4 show how many types of resources each library provided links to on their home page. Table 1 shows this for the libraries with only independent links, and Table 2 for the libraries with two levels of links. (The three libraries which grouped their links in three levels have been counted with the two-level libraries as they only had one relevant category in the highest level [example: Library resources > Additional resources > Subject guides]). Table 3 breaks down the two-level libraries by each link. Table 4 adds Tables 1 and 2 together. The mean (μ) number of links and the Standard deviation (SD) are given for each type. As one could well expect the library's own catalogue to be on its home page, and thus consider it too ubiquitous to bother counting, a second set of data is provided which leaves the catalogue out.

The average number of resources on the ARL libraries' home pages is 7.2 (6.2 not including the catalogue), but this differs whether a library has one level of links or two. If a library has one level of links, it has an average of 4.3 links (3.4 without the catalogue) and if a library has two levels, it has an average of 8.4 links (7.4 without the catalogue). A statistical calculation of the two means using an independent measures *t*-test showed the difference in the mean number of resource links on their home page between the one-level and two-level libraries is signifi-

TABLE 1. Number of electronic resources on the home page of the 33 libraries with one level of links.

# of resources:	0	1	2	3	4	5	6	7	8	9	μ	SD
Including catalogue	0	4	4	4	4	5	7	4	0	1	4.3	2.1
Not including catalogue	1	7	5	3	6	7	4	0	1	0	3.4	2.0

μ = mean number of electronic resources, SD = standard deviation

TABLE 2. Number of electronic resources on the home page of the 81 libraries with two levels of links.

# of resources:	2	3	4	5	6	7	8	9	10	11	12
Incl. catalogue		1	3	7	15	14	12	5	9	5	1
Not incl. catalogue	1	3	7	14	13	12	5	9	5	1	1

# of resources:	13	14	15	16	18	19	20	26	27	μ	SD
Incl. catalogue	1	2	1	1	0	1	1	0	1	8.4	3.8
Not incl. catalogue	2	1	1	0	1	1	0	1		7.4	3.8

μ = mean number of electronic resources, SD = standard deviation

TABLE 3. Number of electronic resources on home page at each level for the 81 libraries with two levels of links.

# of resources:	1	2	3	4	5	6	7	8	9
1st level links, incl. catalogue	17	28	19	8	6	1			
2nd level links, incl. catalogue	6	6	8	10	10	12	8	7	4
1st level links, not incl. catalogue	38	24	11	5	1	1			
2nd level links, not incl. catalogue	7	7	8	13	10	11	9	3	4

# of resources:	10	11	12	13	15	23	24	μ	SD
1st level links, incl. catalogue								2.5	1.2
2nd level links, incl. catalogue	3	1	0	2	2	0	1	5.9	3.7
1st level links, not incl. catalogue								1.9	1.1
2nd level links, not incl. catalogue	2	1	1	1	2	1		5.6	3.6

μ = mean number of electronic resources, SD = standard deviation

TABLE 4. Number of electronic resources on home page for all 114 libraries.

# of resources	0	1	2	3	4	5	6	7	8	9	10	11
Incl. catalogue	0	4	4	5	7	12	22	18	12	6	9	5
Not incl. catalogue	1	7	6	6	13	21	17	12	6	9	5	1
# of resources	12	13	14	15	16	18	19	20	26	27	μ	SD
Incl. catalogue	1	1	2	1	1	0	1	1	0	1	7.2	3.8
Not incl. catalogue	1	2	1	1	0	1	1	0	1		6.2	3.8

μ = mean number of electronic resources, SD = standard deviation

cant and is unlikely to be by chance alone.[2] Two observations were noted that could explain this:

1. The only non-catalogue link in many of the one-level Web pages was "Electronic resources" (or an equivalent phrase), and anyone who wanted a certain resource was obliged to go deeper into the Web site.
2. A library could organize more resources with direct links in a clearer fashion with a two-level Web page, where an equal number of links in a one-level Web page would probably confuse patrons.

There is no relationship between the number of resources on the home pages and the size of the library.[3]

Types of Electronic Resources Available Directly from the Home Page

The types of electronic resources on the ARL libraries' home pages were tallied. The links were tested to see if they led to electronic resources or just a description of them (for example, some libraries had links labelled "Government information" that went to a description of the Government Documents department rather than to links to actual governmental Web sites) and, as different libraries use different wordings, what the resource actually was.

Some libraries had one link labelled with two types of resources where other libraries had two separate links. It was decided to count such links as half one resource and half another, with the exception of links labelled "Databases and e-journals" or the equivalent, which were counted as one link to a general electronic resources area, since other libraries used the phrase "Electronic resources" as a link to a combined databases and e-journals page.

Table 5 is the easiest way to show the result. The numbers may seem surprisingly low in the case of some resources, but this table is not a table of what libraries own, but to what they provide access directly from the home page. For example, many libraries have links to newspapers, but put them deeper in the Web site (such as putting newspapers as a category under "Web reference").

The Catalogue

All the libraries had a catalogue in their Web site, though four did not provide links from their home pages. Many libraries not only provided links on their home page, but also made it possible to search the catalogue directly on the home page. Others had the catalogue further within. Linda A. Rich and Julie L. Rabine have "measured" the distance from a library's home page to its e-journal page, in clicks. ("How Libraries," 42; "Changing Access," 10) A similar measure was taken to measure the distance from the home page to a page where one could conduct a search. Table 6 shows the result, with mean (μ) and standard deviation.

For some sites, accessing the catalogue required hovering with the mouse over some words; these were counted as half a click. Nine libraries designed their catalogues so that an Amazon-style keyword search appeared first. The distance in clicks was reduced for such searches in three libraries from 1 to 0, in two libraries from 2 to 1, in one library from 2 to 0, in one library from 2.5 to 0, and in two libraries from 4 to 3, with the mean thus being reduced to 1.3 and the standard deviation to 0.9. This is not typical practice; as Table 6 shows, the average library has its catalogue within one or two clicks from the home page. There is no correlation between the size of the library and the number of clicks to the catalogue.[4]

Although some libraries may still make use of text-based catalogues, only six provide access to them directly from the home page.

Electronic Resources in General

Complete data from beyond the home page could not be gathered for all of the 114 libraries, as twelve restricted access to institutional users to those parts of the Web site that dealt with electronic resources. How-

TABLE 5. Number of libraries that have a certain type of electronic resource available directly from the home page.

	As a 1st level link	As a 2nd level link	Libraries that have link
Library's own catalogue	81	29	110
Databases/articles/indexes	38	51 1/2	92
E-journals	21	56 1/2	87
E-resources	73	1	74
Subject guides/Research guides	26	36	62
Ready Reference/Web Reference	20	36	56
Catalogues (in general)	17	26	43
E-reserves/Course reserves	19	19	38
E-books	3 1/2	26 1/2	33
Search engines	10	18	28
Digital library/Digital projects	9	18	27
Local catalogue consortium	3	21	24
Government information	2	12	14
Newspapers	1/2	11	13
Worldcat	2	9	11
Statistics	0	11	11
Other libraries	3	6	9
How to do research	2	6	8
Dictionaries	1/2	5	6
Images	1/2	4 1/2	6
Subject guides for specific subjects	0	6	6
Encyclopaedias	1/2	4	5
Geographic information systems	0	4	4
Full-text resources	1	2	3
CRL catalogue	0	3	3
Style manuals	0	3	3
Theses	1	1	2
Associations	0	2	2
Directories	0	2	2
Exams	0	2	2
How to use the Internet	0	2	2
Multiple catalogue searches	0	2	2
Patents	0	2	2
RLIN catalogue	0	2	2
26 other types of resources in one library each			

TABLE 6. Number of clicks to get to the catalogue from the home page.

# of clicks:	0	1/2	1	1 1/2	2	2 1/2	3	4	μ	SD
# of libraries	18	1	45	2	34	1	10	3	1.4	1.0

μ = mean number of clicks, SD = standard deviation

ever, only two of these had a complete ban on outside access for any type of electronic resource whatsoever. The other ten put their restrictions in varying places so that in some cases one could find out basic information, such as that the library had databases, even if one could not find out which databases they had.

Most libraries separated their electronic resources into categories; few lumped their resources into one list (or provided access to such an unsorted list), whether the list was available as one big list (5, 4.4%) or as a list in alphabetical parts with a link to each letter (9, 7.9%). The two types of lists are not necessarily exclusive; many libraries provided both types for different categories of resources.

Somewhat more (19, 16.7%) had a search engine of all electronic resources to find individual ones. In addition, twenty-two (19.3%) provided subject access to all of their electronic resources (i.e., choosing a subject will generate a list of all electronic resources dealing with the subject). Eleven of these went further and provided two levels of subjects; the average number of subjects in the first level was 7.2[5] and in the second level was 64.9.[6] The one-level subject libraries provided an average of 56.4 subjects.[7] One other library had three levels of 3, 12, and 111 subjects each. The average number of subjects used was 66.7.[8] In short, most libraries seemed to consider that their users look for a certain type of resource first rather than any electronic resource on a subject.

Databases

One hundred and one libraries (87.8%) had separate access to databases somewhere in their Web site, such as a separate database page or a link that provided a search engine to databases only. Fifty-nine (51.8%) had one list of all databases, 42 (36.8%) had alphabetical part-lists, and 30 (26.3%) had a search engine of database names. Twenty-eight (24.6%) provided separate lists of frequently used databases and 19 (16.7%) to full-text databases. Twelve (10.5%) categorized their databases by type; they used an average of 8.8 types.[9]

Table 7 gives two measurements of distance to databases from the home page. The first is the distance either to a database itself, more specifically a database whose title began with the letter A (usually ABI Inform) as many libraries which provided part-lists had the "A" list as the default list, or to a screen which required a login. The assumption made was that after a successful login, the library's user would be taken to the database in question with the next screen. The second measurement is in conformity with Rich and Rabine's method of measuring the distance to the resource type page (here the database page). ("How Libraries," 42; "Changing Access," 10) Here too, some databases were reached via a mouse hover that caused further links to appear; this was counted as half a click. There is no correlation between the library's size and the distance of a database.[10]

Electronic Journals

Ninety-two libraries (80.7%) had separate access to e-journals somewhere in their Web site. Nineteen (16.7%) had one list of all e-journals, 62 (54.4%) had alphabetical part-lists (unsurprisingly, there are more part-lists as complete e-journal lists would get very large and unwieldy to maintain or look at), and 60 (52.6%) had a search engine of e-journal names.

Thirty-six (31.6%) made some use of the catalogue to find e-journals. Nineteen libraries (16.7%) referred to their catalogue as an alternative way of searching for the library's e-journals, while in seventeen libraries (14.9%), the catalogue was the exclusive way of searching for the library's e-journals.

Twenty-seven (23.7%) provided links to individual collections of e-journals (grouped by publisher) and seven (6.1%) provided links to "full-text journals." Thirty-five libraries (30.7%) provided subject access; one had three levels of 3, 12, and 111 subjects, seven (7.0%) had two levels of subjects, and twenty-seven (23.7%) one level of subjects. The average number of first-level subjects was 6.9[11] and of second-level subjects was 55.1.[12] The one-level libraries provided an average of 53.5 subjects,[13] and the average number of subjects for all the libraries was 57.3.[14]

Table 8 provides a similar method of distance to Table 7. It is interesting to compare the figures in the third row to Rich and Rabine's, measured in 2000, which gave an average distance of 1.4 clicks (stan-

TABLE 7. Number of clicks to get to the databases from the home page.

# of clicks:	0	1	1 1/2	2	2 1/2	3	3 1/2	4	4 1/2	5	n	μ	SD
To a database			1	12	7	42	3	35	3	2	105	3.3	0.7
To database pages	2	76	14	9							101	1.1	0.4

n = total number of libraries, μ = mean number of clicks, SD = standard deviation

TABLE 8. Number of clicks to get to the e-journals from the home page.

# of clicks:	0	1	1 1/2	2	2 1/2	3	3 1/2	4	4 1/2	5	6	8	n	μ	SD
To an e-journal				2	2	36	7	34	4	14	1	1	101	3.8	0.9
To e-journal pages	2	61	13	15		1							92	1.2	0.5

n = total number of libraries, μ = mean number of clicks, SD = standard deviation

dard deviation 0.5) for 105 libraries. ("Changing Access, 42) There is no correlation between the size of the library and the number of clicks to an e-journal.[15]

Ready Reference

Seventy-one libraries (62.3%) provided links to Web sites useful for ready reference. Most of these (60, 52.6%) arranged their reference sites by type of information needed (such as dictionaries and telephone numbers), with an average of 26.0 types. Far fewer (16, 14.0%) arranged the reference sites by subject. Most libraries did not arrange such Web sites in a list, whether one big list (13, 11.4%) or alphabetical part-lists (3, 2.6%). Sixty-two libraries (54.4%) provided online chat reference for an average of 44 hours 20 minutes a week. (Two libraries were part of a worldwide consortium that provided online chat reference for all hours of the week; if one factors these out as not being the library's own service the average drops to 39 hours 55 minutes.)

Other

Sixty-six libraries (57.9%) provided research guides arranged by subject, fifty-five (48.2%) in one level (with an average of 58.5 subjects) and eleven (9.6%) in two levels of subjects (with an average of 9.1 subjects in the first level and 64.2 in the second level). Twenty libraries (17.5%) had government information somewhere on their Web site (which is not the same as a link to the library's Government Documents department). Sixteen libraries (14.0%) had statistics pages, 34 (29.8%) had links to e-book collections, 22 (19.3%) had separate links to newspapers collections (i.e., not buried in the ready reference links), 31 (27.2%) provided links to Internet search engines, and 18 (15.8%) provided their students with advice on how to do research.

WHAT DO LIBRARIES DO WITH ELECTRONIC RESOURCES IN THEIR CATALOGUE?

During March 2003, a sample group of ten electronic resources was searched for in the catalogues of all 114 academic ARL libraries to examine the ARL libraries' broad cataloguing practice for such resources, i.e., whether they are put into the catalogue or not. It was considered that ten resources would be sufficient to determine what such a broad practice was, or whether there even was a practice.

The resources were selected from a list of electronic resources currently subscribed to at the author's institution (University of Oklahoma), and were chosen with the assistance of one of the reference librarians there. The criteria used to select a resource were:

1. it was thought likely to be a common tool most of the ARL libraries would have, whether in electronic form or paper form, and therefore direct comparisons could be made, and;
2. there was a simple one-to-one equivalency between the paper form and the electronic form (the electronic form was the electronic version of only one paper resource and not a combination of many paper resources, such as GeoRef). Therefore for a given electronic resource only one paper resource would need to be searched for and compared with in the catalogue and the question "Does this library own this resource?" could be answered with a simple Yes or No.

Eight resources were items that are usually catalogued as serials, although only one was a "pure" serial that the public would easily recognize as such. Five of these were indexes, and two were tools generally used only by librarians (and were chosen on the assumption that a tool for librarians would certainly be an item that academic libraries would hold). The remaining two were monographs.

The paper versions of the resources were:

1. *Books in Print*. New York: Bowker, 1948- .
2. *Historical Abstracts: Bibliography of the World's Literature*. Santa Barbara, CA: ABC-Clio, 2001- . Its former two parts, *Modern History Abstracts 1775-1914* and *Twentieth Century Abstracts, 1914-2000* were considered equivalent, since no library was likely to have one without the other.
3. *Library Literature & Information Science (Cumulation)*. New York: H. W. Wilson, 2000- , or its former title *Library Literature*.
4. *MLA International Bibliography of Books and Articles on the Modern Languages and Literatures*. Library ed. New York: Modern Language Association of America, 1970- .
5. *Nature*. London: Macmillan, 1869- .
6. *The New Encyclopaedia Britannica*. Chicago: Encyclopaedia Britannica, 2002, or any other recent edition, "recent" being very broadly defined as "within the last ten years," the existence of the electronic version obviating the need to keep the most current paper copy.
7. *The Oxford English Dictionary*. 2nd ed. Oxford: Clarendon Press, 1989. This was specifically chosen to test whether libraries would go back and edit the record for the paper version to provide access to the electronic version.
8. *The Philosopher's Index*. Bowling Green, OH: Philosophy Documentation Center, Bowling Green University, 1967- .
9. *Ulrich's Periodicals Directory*. New Providence, NJ: Bowker, 2001- , or its former title *Ulrich's International Periodicals Directory*.
10. *The Zoological Record*. London: J. V. Voorst, 1870- .

Some of the paper resources have multiple electronic versions. However, it was not considered important to note which electronic version a library had, for they all shared the fundamental characteristic of being an electronic version of a paper resource and therefore all electronic versions were held to be equivalent.

Two academic libraries (George Washington University and the University of Georgia) did not have a database list open to outsiders, and therefore, they were discarded as not being able to provide a useful result. As there were 112 academic libraries left, 1,120 resources were thus searched for.

Methods of Providing Access to Electronic Resources

The dichotomy of "a library does/does not put its electronic resource into the catalogue" was found to be insufficient to take into account such factors as the presence or absence of a resource in the catalogue, the presence of it in a directory on the Web page instead, the presence or absence of the 856 field (URL) in the paper version of the resource (which appears in the public catalogue as a link to the resource), and (since most of the resources examined were serials) whether the library currently subscribed to the paper version of the serial. In fact, ten categories were needed, of which all but the last two can be considered a method of providing access to electronic resources (which leaves 954 records). For each category the number and percentage of the whole and of the access-providing methods are given.

A. The library owns both the print and electronic versions, has separate records for both, but links in neither (4 records, 0.4% [0.4%] of the total). One may wonder what the use of a record for an electronic version is without a URL and why any library would use such a method of indicating it owns a certain electronic resource. However, the tiny number of records in this category seems to indicate that this practice is the result of a mistake more than anything else, since two of the records were incomplete and one was marked on order. (The fourth was marked "ask at desk," which may point to an older CD-ROM that cannot be used on a network.)

B. The library owns both versions, has separate records for both, with the link in the online version only (316 records, 28.2% [33.1%] of the total). This was the most common category. The assumption here is that in an electronic age, patrons who look in a record for a print version purposefully want the print version, and if they wanted a link to take them to the electronic version, they would have looked in the record for the electronic version. This could also indicate the library does not go back and edit the records for the print versions.

C. The library owns both versions, has separate records for both, but links in both records (138 records, 12.3% [14.5%] of the total). The assumption here is that the electronic version is so important (or popular) that a library should provide links to it everywhere it can.

D. The library owns both versions and has one common record (219 records, 19.6% [23.0%] of the total). The assumption here is that there is no especial difference between the two versions since patrons will use both for the same thing (though perhaps the convenience of the electronic version will make it the more favoured of the two). As the second-most used category, this was often used to provide a link in a paper version cancelled long ago.

E. The library owns both, but the online version is not in the catalogue (87 records, 7.8% [9.1%] of the total). The assumption here is that patrons who want the electronic version will not bother to search in a catalogue for it, but prefer to consult lists.

F. The library owns both, but online version (which is in the catalogue) is the current version (81 records, 7.2% [8.5%] of the total). Because serials can be cancelled at any time, "current" was arbitrarily defined to mean that the print version was less than ten years old, for though a serial cancelled within the past few years may presumably be suspended for budget cuts and re-acquired when money is not so tight, it is unlikely that a library will bother to re-subscribe to a serial cancelled ten years ago. Any serial cancelled more than ten years ago was considered equivalent to the library not owning it.

G. The library owns only the online version, which is in the catalogue (72 records, 6.4% [7.5%] of the total). The assumption here is that everything a library owns should be in the catalogue.

H. The library owns only the online version, which is not in the catalogue (37 records, 3.3% [3.9%] of the total). The assumption here is the same as in E.

I. The library owns the print version only (130 records, 11.6% of the total).

J. The library owns neither version (36 records, 3.2% of the total). Twenty-four of these were libraries that did not own *Zoological Record*. A recalculation of the figures minus *Zoological Record* showed little change in proportion.

These finer categories, though, can be compacted into the dichotomy mentioned above as follows: resources with catalogue access (B+C+D+F+G), 826 records, 73.8%; resources without catalogue access (A+E+H), 128 records, 11.4%; other situations (I+J), 166 records,

14.8%. Discarding the "other situations" as not being relevant to electronic resources, this gives a total of 86.6% with catalogue access and 13.4% without. Therefore, one can answer the broad question of "Do libraries put their electronic resources in the catalogue?" with Yes.

(Percentage figures concerning the records from here on will be given in terms of the 954 records that are relevant to electronic resources.)

Of the finer categories, only three of the resources had a method the majority of libraries used. For both versions of *Nature*, 64.4% of libraries (67) had one record [category D]. Assuredly the print version of the journal was downloaded into their catalogues long before the Internet became commonly known, so this is an obvious sign that some libraries have gone back to edit their print records in some situations (though whether the editing is done by themselves or by a service such as Serials Solutions cannot be determined in this paper), especially as a further 15.4% (16) of libraries had URLs in both versions [category C].

However, not as many libraries do this as one would think by examining *Nature* alone. Of the ten resources chosen, only *Nature* had a majority of edited records: the rest ranged from 46.6% (*Ulrich's*, which has a URL in its record for the newest print version) to a low of 13.0% (*Britannica*) with the total being 37.4% (357 records). The more common practice is to simply download a record for the electronic version [categories B, F and G], with 49.2% of records (469) being downloaded in this way. Three resources have a majority of such records, and four a plurality over print records with URLs.

The other two resources that had a majority practice were *Britannica*, which had separate records with no link to the print version in 71.4% of libraries (55) and *The Oxford English Dictionary*, which had separate records in 67.3% (66). For the dictionary, the inference that the majority of libraries refrain from going back to re-edit their print records would be enough to explain this (for the print version was published in 1989). For *Britannica*, it is very likely also because the only print record on OCLC in the past 10 years that has a URL link is the 1993 record.

No library used the same method, either for all ten resources or for that portion of the ten they owned. Twelve libraries used two methods, 40 used three, 37 used four, 18 used five, and 5 used six (the average number of methods used therefore being 3.6). The two most consistent libraries were the University of Delaware (7/8, 88% using method B with the remainder method D) and Ohio State University (7/8, 88% using method B with the remainder method C). Of the libraries that owned 9 resources, New York University (7/9, 78% using method D with the remainder method B), and University of Texas at Austin (7/9, 78% using method D with one resource using method B and one method G) were the most consistent. Of the libraries that owned 10 resources, Cornell University (8/10, 80% using method B with the remainder method C) and Ohio University (8/10, 80% using method C with one method B and one method E) were the most consistent. Three other libraries (University of Massachusetts, Syracuse University, and University of Houston) used one method over 75% of the time.

One can draw no conclusion, though, as to whether or not individual libraries have decided upon a method of access. Although the consistency within some libraries' catalogues may be a sign that some libraries devised policies of catalogue access from the start and have stuck with it, one cannot hold the variation in other libraries' catalogues to mean that they have no policy. Because different libraries may have acquired different electronic resources at different times, the variation may simply reflect historical variation in their policies. One would need to specifically search for the most recently catalogued electronic resources to determine the presence or absence of a policy.

In terms of the dichotomy of "electronic resources do/do not have catalogue access), there was much more consistency. Fifty-six of the 112 academic libraries surveyed had catalogue access for 100% of the resources examined (that they owned), and thirty-two of them had catalogue access for 75% or over. One library (University of Southern California) was consistent in that 75% of the resources examined were *not* in the catalogue.

In all, 104 libraries had catalogue access for a majority of the ten resources examined that they owned, four libraries were evenly split, and four did not have catalogue access for a majority of the ten resources that they owned. Therefore, it is safe to generalize that academic libraries provide access to electronic resources through the catalogue, although the exact method of doing so in individual libraries may differ.

NOTES

1. The largest library had 14,685,926 volumes; the smallest, 1,514,113; with a mean = 3,724,075; median = 2,909,643; and standard deviation = 2,163,416. There are 100 American libraries and 14 Canadian libraries.

2. $t = 2.38$ for the means with the catalog, and 2.59 for the means without the catalog, which is significantly different even at $\alpha = .01$.

3. Comparing the number of volumes held by a library and the number of links to electronic resources on the home page with the Pearson correlation give a value of $r = +0.14$.

4. A Pearson correlation gives the value $r = -0.05$.

5. Minimum 3, maximum 13, standard deviation 3.1.

6. Minimum 12, maximum 117, standard deviation 27.1.

7. Minimum 10, maximum 114, standard deviation 27.7.

8. Minimum 10, maximum 128, standard deviation 31.4.

9. Minimum 4, maximum 14, standard deviation 2.6.

10. The Pearson correlation gives $r = +0.02$.

11. Minimum 3, maximum 12, standard deviation 2.7.

12. Minimum 24, maximum 84, standard deviation 16.5.

13. Minimum 4, maximum 268, standard deviation 52.8.

14. Minimum 4, maximum 268, standard deviation 48.6.

15. The Pearson correlation gives $r = -0.02$.

REFERENCES

Chaudhry, Abdus Sattar, and Makeswary Periasamy. "A Study of Current Practices of Selected Libraries in Cataloguing Electronic Journals." *Library Review* 50.9 (2001): 434-443.

Kirkwood, Hal P., Jr. "Business Library Web Sites: A Review of the Organization and Structure of Print, Networked, and Internet Resources." *Journal of Business & Finance Librarianship* 5.4 (2001): 23-37.

Osorio, Nestor L. "Web Sites of Science-Engineering Libraries: An Analysis of Content and Design." *Issues in Science and Technology Librarianship* 29 (2001) 2 April 2003. http://www.istl.org/01-winter/refereed.html.

Owen, D.B. *Handbook of Statistical Tables.* Reading, Mass.: Addison-Wesley, 1962.

Rich, Linda A. and Julie L. Rabine. "The Changing Access to Electronic Journals: A Survey of Academic Library Websites Revisited." *Serials Review* 27.3-4 (2001): 1-16.

_____. "A Comparison of Research University and Two-Year College Library Web Sites: Content, Functionality, and Form." *College & Research Libraries* 60.3 (1999): 275-289.

_____. "How Libraries Are Providing Access to Electronic Serials: A Survey of Academic Library Web Sites." *Serials Review* 25.2 (1999): 35-46.

Riemer, John J. "CONSER's Aggregator Survey and the Work of the PCC Task Group." *Cataloging & Classification Quarterly* 28.4 (1999): 7-13.

Still, Julie M. "A Content Analysis of University Library Web Sites in English Speaking Countries." *Online Information Review* 25.3 (2001): 160-164.

The Changing Format
of Reference Collections:
Are Research Libraries Favoring
Electronic Access over Print?

Sarah Robbins
Cheryl McCain
Laurie Scrivener

SUMMARY. This study examines the holdings of ARL libraries for core reference titles to see if there is a trend towards canceling the print in favor of electronic, and discusses the implications of duplication of titles in both formats. It also looks at the issue within the context of several areas of study including general reference, arts and humanities, social sciences, and sciences. *[Article copies available for a fee from The Haworth Document Delivery Service: 1-800-HAWORTH. E-mail address: <docdelivery@haworthpress.com> Website: <http://www.HaworthPress.com> © 2006 by The Haworth Press, Inc. All rights reserved.]*

Sarah Robbins is Electronic Services Coordinator (E-mail: srobbins@ou.edu); Cheryl McCain is Acquisitions Librarian (E-mail: clmccain@ou.edu); and Laurie Scrivener is Social Sciences Reference Librarian (E-mail: lscrivener@ou.edu), all at the University of Oklahoma Libraries, 401 West Brooks, Norman, OK 73019.

[Haworth co-indexing entry note]: "The Changing Format of Reference Collections: Are Research Libraries Favoring Electronic Access over Print?" Robbins, Sarah, Cheryl McCain, and Laurie Scrivener. Co-published simultaneously in *The Acquisitions Librarian* (The Haworth Information Press, an imprint of The Haworth Press, Inc.) No. 35/36, 2006, pp. 75-95; and: *Integrating Print and Digital Resources in Library Collections* (ed: Audrey Fenner) The Haworth Information Press, an imprint of The Haworth Press, Inc., 2006, pp. 75-95. Single or multiple copies of this article are available for a fee from The Haworth Document Delivery Service [1-800-HAWORTH, 9:00 a.m. - 5:00 p.m. (EST). E-mail address: docdelivery@haworthpress.com].

Available online at http://www.haworthpress.com/web/AL
© 2006 by The Haworth Press, Inc. All rights reserved.

Digital Object Identifier: 10.1300/J101v18n35_06

KEYWORDS. Academic libraries, electronic resources, reference materials, collection development

INTRODUCTION

With the increasing popularity of Web-based access to traditional library resources, librarians are being challenged to balance user demands for the new technologies with their duty as custodians of information. They must make information accessible to current users in the format they prefer, while insuring that it will be available to future generations. Purchasing print, a proven archival medium, and electronic versions of the same title can easily consume libraries' budgets. Librarians must ask themselves whether it is worthwhile to purchase a seldom used print copy of a title for archival purposes when the library is also paying for more heavily used electronic access to the same title.

Reference collection budgets have been hit particularly hard by the increasing availability of electronic resources. Indexing and abstracting services are well-suited to the electronic format, and electronic indexes are usually preferred over their print counterparts. Other reference materials such as encyclopedias, handbooks, dictionaries, and directories are also increasingly available in an electronic format, although preference for print versus electronic of this type of source is less certain. Regardless, libraries often purchase both types of electronic reference sources, even in the face of declining budgets. Subject specialists and reference collection developers must make tough decisions in regard to canceling a print version of a reference title and relying solely on the electronic version.

Although this is an issue faced by libraries everywhere, little research has been done to determine what action libraries are actually taking. This study examines trends among leading North American research libraries in canceling the print versions of core general, arts and humanities, social science, and science reference titles, in favor of electronic access to the same sources. Research libraries were chosen as the sample population because they are depended upon to archive materials for future generations, yet they must also meet current users' expectations and accommodate users' preferences for electronic access.

LITERATURE REVIEW

Electronic resources have had a significant impact on the way librarians select materials and budget for them, and the literature reflects this. Much has been written about the nature of electronic collections, selection criteria for this relatively new format, and the impact of electronic collections on library budgets.

Electronic resources create unique challenges for librarians in the area of collection development. A recurrent theme in discussions about the prevalence of online reference titles is the generalization of reference collections. Landesman notes,

> It is difficult to see how collections can offer the breadth of title selection that they did in print. Foreign titles, out-of-print titles, and titles from smaller publishers have suffered in print collections and, as on-going costs for serials escalate, libraries fear they are producing 'vanilla' collections which are very similar to each other. ("Sense" 82)

When asked how decisions about format were made, Christopher Nolan at Trinity University responded, "[T]here is pressure to spend our money on high-visibility, high-use general sources and not spend it on traditional printed products that are often more specialized. [. . .] [W]e may also be getting more use out of those high visibility sources" (Wilkinson, "Reference Materials–Where Formats" 16). This pressure threatens the very nature of the traditional research library's reference collection. If money is spent on general titles, there is necessarily less money for other more specialized titles.

Print allows librarians to pick and choose individual titles based on the needs of a library's users, while, as Holleman notes, "librarians cannot shape the contents of an electronic product for their own constituencies" (Holleman 695). Librarians select databases that they feel best suit the needs of their users, but information contained within these databases is left to the publisher's discretion and could change without notice. Kluegel compares the changes in reference collections as a result of the addition of electronic collections to a kaleidoscope; collections change daily and users are never sure what they are going to see ("Reference" 10). A printed book does not change after it is purchased–chapters are not deleted nor are graphics suddenly omitted. This type of sustainability is not guaranteed with electronic products.

Consortial purchasing, while necessary to increase the buying power of a library's finite budget, contributes to the generalization of collections. As libraries continue to participate in consortial agreements, there is a shift from local control of the collections to a reliance on consortial participation (Kluegel, "Revolutionary" 454). A librarian from the University of New Mexico notes, "As libraries increasingly acquire commercial databases and other resources that are used for reference purposes via consortial licenses (e.g., FirstSearch), reference departments will no longer be the direct managers of these types of resources. They will have less control over adding or dropping a reference database that now may be part of a larger database package negotiated by a library" (Wilkinson, "Reference Materials–To Web" 24). In essence, libraries may pay for information not needed by their users in order to receive discounted prices on other products they actually need.

Archiving electronic information to insure access to future generations is a concern of many librarians. Many fear that what is here today may be gone tomorrow, and libraries would have nothing to show for their years of paying for access to a given resource. Okerson explains, "The fear is that information which has lost its commercial value may disappear if left in the hands of commercial [. . .] owners only; but there is yet no model for transferring control and responsibility to any not-for-profit entity or group of entities" (682). Davis warns selectors to "never assume that this responsibility is safe in the hands of database producers. Publishers have not traditionally maintained paper stock, and they have quickly realized that they are not in the business of storing large sets of data and maintaining ready access to them" (398). Many factors could contribute to the demise of an electronic product. One librarian notes, "Mergers, the expense of archiving information indefinitely, decisions to delete an old database in order to save space, replacing a first edition with a second, the demise of an electronic publisher–any of these would terminate access" (Wilkinson, "Reference Materials–To Web" 20). When faculty members in the social sciences were interviewed about their preferences between print and electronic resources, one faculty member cautioned that "the electronics are nothing but these little magnetic blips and blops" (Palmer and Sandler 27).

Duplication of titles is another factor that must be considered when making decisions about whether or not to continue acquiring the print version of a title when electronic access is also available. Schmitt suggests that duplicating titles in both formats is making "a choice not to buy something we don't already own" and warns that "[o]ur collections become shallower, less diverse, less well-rounded" when libraries make such decisions (26). In the article "Reference Materials–Where Formats and Budget Lines Collide: Librarians Speak Out," librarians were asked about duplication of resources within their collections due to multiple formats. Most of the librarians responded that duplication is typically minimized by canceling the print once the electronic format becomes available, if pricing structures and licensing requirements support this decision. Reasons given for continued duplication include: bundling of the print and electronic products, restrictive licenses that prevent a public university from providing walk-in access to the electronic version, and a distrust of electronic information's stability (Wilkinson 16, 18).

METHODOLOGY

Forty-five key reference titles that are available both in print and electronically were selected using *Gale Directory of Databases* and Katz's *Introduction to Reference Work: Volume I, Basic Information Sources*. After initial searching in the catalogs of several sample libraries, seven titles were removed from this list, leaving 38 titles to be examined throughout the study (see Appendix). The seven titles were removed from the list for a variety of reasons. For one of the titles, the most recent print edition was more than a couple of years old, and therefore, the question of whether or not it was currently being received in print did not apply. Several of the ready reference titles could effectively be replaced by the Internet; thus, there was no way to measure whether or not a library canceled the print version in favor of an electronic equivalent. Other titles removed were deemed too narrow in scope to be applicable to the curriculum of the majority of research libraries.

Each of the reference titles was placed into one of four categories–general reference, arts and humanities, social sciences, or sciences. These categories were used to determine trends among the various areas of study in regard to canceling print copies of a title in favor of the electronic version of the same title.

From January to March 2003, catalogs and lists of electronic holdings for the 114 libraries belonging to the Association of Research Libraries (ARL) that are also affiliated with an institution of higher education were examined. Public and special libraries that are members of ARL were not included in this study.

Each catalog was searched for the selected reference titles and the last year a given title was received in print was noted. Due to inconsistencies among catalogs in the way holdings are displayed, some assumptions were made. First, if a record's holdings indicated a starting date followed by a hyphen (e.g., 1967-), the holdings were recorded as "to date" rather than as a year. Second, if a record used terminology that indicated the title was "currently received," the holdings were also recorded as "to date." Third, if there was a record in the catalog for a print title but holdings were indiscernible, the holdings were listed simply as "yes" rather than as a year. If no record for a title could be found in the online catalog, it was assumed that the library did not carry the title in print and holdings were recorded as "no."

Both a library's online catalog and its Web page listings of electronic holdings were examined to determine the availability of electronic access to the reference titles for each library. Electronic holdings were recorded as "yes" if an institution had online access to a title and as "no" if an institution did not have online access to the title. If an institution only had retrospective electronic access to a title, this was also recorded as a "no" since the purpose of this study is to see if institutions are ceasing to receive current print titles when an electronic equivalent is available. An electronic resource had to be available online rather than merely on CD-ROM for it to qualify as having electronic access.

After the data were accumulated, four more titles were excluded from the study, bringing the final count of reference titles examined to 34. In order to assure its significance to academic ARL libraries, a title had to be owned by at least 85% of the institutions examined. Using this criterion, *The Grove Dictionary of Art* was dropped from the study as only 82% of the institutions studied owned either the most recent edition or a past edition of the title. *The Book Review Index* is available through mediated searching, but most libraries do not provide electronic access to this title; thus, its data were also removed from the overall analysis. *The New York Times Index* and *Communication Abstracts* were also dropped from the overall analysis due to the fact that the titles can be electronically accessed through multiple sources that were not easily identifiable.

SUMMARY OF FINDINGS

Overview

As noted in the methodology, the last year a resource was received in print, as denoted in the catalog holdings for each library, was recorded.

The data were then combined at the title level so that a cumulative record of when a title was last received by all of the libraries studied could be viewed. From this, a percentage was calculated and graphed showing when titles were last received in print, by area of study to which the titles belonged (see Figure 1). Percentages were used for comparison since different numbers of titles were examined for each category. For the purposes of the graph, the number of records indicating that a title was received "to date" was incorporated into the number of titles last received in 2003.

By looking at the information presented in Figure 1, one can see that the percentage of holdings in the general reference category in 2003 is more than double the percentage of holdings for the arts and humanities, social sciences, or sciences for the same year. The percentage of print holdings last received in the arts and humanities and social sciences peaked in 2001 while the percentage of science titles received in print peaked in 2002 and 2003. Several of the social sciences and arts and humanities titles studied (*Current Index to Journals in Education: CIJE, Resources in Education: RIE, Mental Measurements Yearbook*, and *New Grove Dictionary of Music and Musicians*) were either last published in 2001 or the most recent edition available was in 2001. This may explain why the social sciences and arts and humanities areas peaked during this year. Throughout the nineties, the latest year of print holdings for all four categories remained under 13%. This indicates that the shift from print access only to electronic access only is gradual and that libraries are still in the midst of making such decisions.

Differences Among Areas of Study

To examine the trend in print holdings of indexing and abstracting titles in the three major areas of study, the general category was removed from Figure 1. The data set for the ready reference titles was excluded as well so that only data for indexing and abstracting titles were included (see Figure 2). Ready reference titles were defined as titles one would use to find a specific piece of information or fact rather than use to find citations to articles or other materials.

Figure 2 shows that for the indexing and abstracting titles there is little difference among the areas of study as far as the percentage of holdings last received in any given year. Even for the years depicting the greatest difference on the graph, there is less than a 10% difference in the percentage of holdings. Among the areas of study, the science hold-

FIGURE 1. Print Reference Source Holdings, by Area of Study

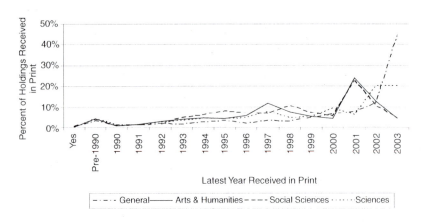

FIGURE 2. Print Index and Abstract Holdings, by Area of Study

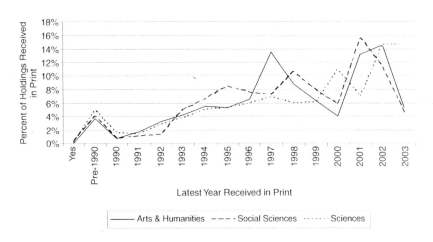

ings have the greatest percentage currently received in print, with approximately 15% of the holdings still being received in 2002 as well as in 2003. Approximately 11% of the social sciences holdings and 14% of the arts and humanities holdings were still being received in print in 2002. In 2003, those percentages dropped to 5% for both the social sciences for the arts and humanities.

Duplication

One of the purposes of this study was to identify libraries maintaining print subscriptions to titles they also receive electronically. To do this, the number of libraries currently receiving print versions of the selected titles was tabulated. (For the purposes of this discussion, an institution had to receive the title in 2002-2003 or have a note in the catalog record indicating that the title is currently being received to be considered as currently receiving a title.) From this subset of data, the number of libraries also receiving the titles in electronic form was calculated. Percentages of the number of libraries receiving both formats were calculated and graphed (see Figure 3). *Resources in Education: RIE* and *Current Index to Journals in Education: CIJE* were not included in Figure 3 since the titles are no longer available in print, and thus, libraries cannot be duplicating them in both print and electronic formats.

By looking at Figure 3, one sees that only seven of the 34 titles examined (*Books in Print, Index Medicus, CRC: Handbook of Chemistry and Physics, New Grove Dictionary of Music and Musicians, Mathematical Reviews*, and *Ulrich's Periodicals Directory, RILM Abstracts of Music Literature*) are currently being duplicated in both the print and online format by more than 50% of the libraries studied. Of these seven titles, three are indexes, while the other four are ready reference resources.

The data presented in Figure 3 were used to examine the number of titles being duplicated in print and electronic format by area of study. The data were examined first with an additional category for the ready reference titles, which was created by extracting these titles from the various areas of study (see Figure 4), and then with the ready reference titles incorporated into the areas of study (see Figure 5). Many of the ready reference titles are still heavily duplicated in both print and electronic formats and do not necessarily have a regular publication cycle like the indexing and abstracting titles.

By examining the information presented in Figure 4, one can see that only one arts and humanities title, two science titles, and four ready reference titles are duplicated in both the print and electronic format by more than 50% of the libraries. In the arts and humanities, social sciences, and sciences, the majority of the titles studied were being duplicated by less than 30% of all the libraries. Only in the ready reference category is there a majority of titles being duplicated by more than 30% of the libraries.

FIGURE 3. Duplication of Reference Sources, by Title

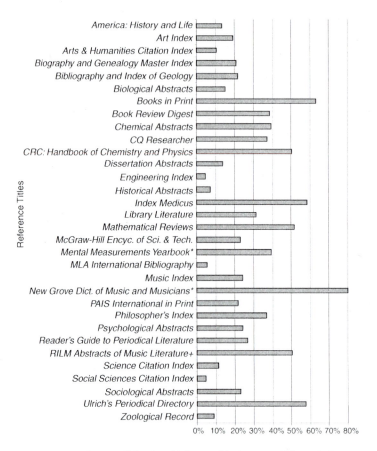

Percent of Libraries with Current Print Issues and Electronic Access

*The year used to calculate libraries with the current print edition of the *New Grove Dictionary of Music and Musicians* and *Mental Measurements Yearbook* was 2001 since that is when they were last published.
+The years used to calculate libraries with the current print edition of *RILM Abstracts of Music Literature* were 1997-1998 since these years were the most current for this title.

When the ready reference materials are incorporated into the areas of study to which they best correspond, it is interesting to note how the numbers do not significantly change (see Figure 5). Three areas–arts and humanities, sciences, and general–have titles being duplicated in the print and electronic format by more than 50% of the libraries. How-

FIGURE 4. Duplication of Reference Sources, by Area of Study (Ready Reference Titles Extracted)

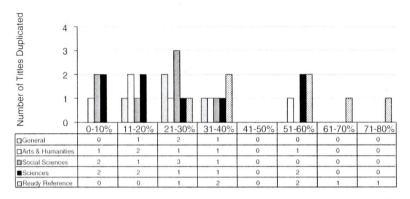

	0-10%	11-20%	21-30%	31-40%	41-50%	51-60%	61-70%	71-80%
☐General	0	1	2	1	0	0	0	0
☐Arts & Humanities	1	2	1	1	0	1	0	0
☒Social Sciences	2	1	3	1	0	0	0	0
■Sciences	2	2	1	1	0	2	0	0
☐Ready Reference	0	0	1	2	0	2	1	1

Percent of Libraries with Duplication

FIGURE 5. Duplication of Reference Sources, by Area of Study

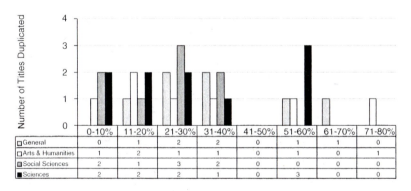

	0-10%	11-20%	21-30%	31-40%	41-50%	51-60%	61-70%	71-80%
☐General	0	1	2	2	0	1	1	0
☐Arts & Humanities	1	2	1	1	0	1	0	1
☒Social Sciences	2	1	3	2	0	0	0	0
■Sciences	2	2	2	1	0	3	0	0

Percent of Libraries with Duplication

ever, as depicted in Figure 4, four of the seven titles falling in this range are ready reference materials rather than indexing or abstracting resources. Even after incorporating the ready reference materials into the other categories, it still holds true that the majority of the titles for the arts and humanities, social sciences, and sciences are duplicated in the print and electronic format by less than 30% of the libraries.

Analysis of Citation Index Holdings

Looking at the citation indexes as a subset of the bigger picture allows detailed examination of the trends of a reference title from each of the areas of study. These titles lend themselves to comparison because the same title is available in the three areas of study, and they serve the same function within each area. They are also all available online in the same database (*Web of Science*). As depicted in Figure 6, the late nineties saw a large decline in the number of libraries receiving print versions of the ISI's citation indexes. Prior to the year 2000, most libraries had stopped receiving the citation indexes in print, with 78 (68%) of the libraries no longer receiving *Arts and Humanities Citation Index*, 86 (75%) of the libraries no longer receiving *Social Sciences Citation Index*, and 82 (72%) of the libraries no longer receiving *Science Citation Index*. The latest year of holdings for all three indexes occurred most often during the years 1997 and 1998.

As of 2002, 13 (11%) of the libraries studied are still receiving the print *Arts & Humanities Citation Index*; six (5%) of the libraries are still receiving the print *Social Sciences Citation Index*; and 14 (12%) of the libraries are still receiving the print *Science Citation Index*. At the same time, 96% of the 114 libraries in this study are receiving online access to each of the citation indexes. The data show that 11% of the libraries are currently receiving *Arts & Humanities Citation Index* and *Science Citation Index* in both the print and electronic format, while only 4% of the

FIGURE 6. Citation Indexes, Print Holdings

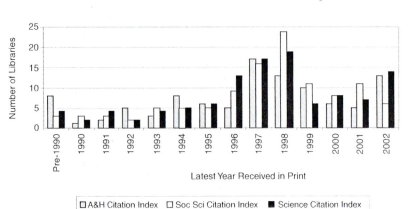

Latest Year Received in Print

□ A&H Citation Index   □ Soc Sci Citation Index   ■ Science Citation Index

libraries are currently receiving *Social Sciences Citation Index* in both formats. It is interesting to note that these three sources have not been handled in the same way regarding cancellation of the print and reliance on the online format only.

Limitations of the Study

In the process of compiling the data for this study, several unanticipated problems were encountered in using and interpreting the various libraries' catalogs. Holdings are not consistently displayed from one library to the next. Some libraries list each issue of a title received, others list only cumulative volumes, while still others note "currently received" or leave an open-ended hyphen to indicate a current subscription. Also, because of the time of year the study was done, it was too early to determine whether a title was no longer received in 2002 unless a catalog record indicated this was the case. In some instances, the date originally recorded as the last date a title was received by a given library was inaccurate by the time follow-up information was gathered because the library had received a more recent volume. Thus, it is apparent that the data are constantly changing.

The study also did not take into consideration the libraries with multiple branches canceling some, but not all, of their print holdings; the latest date a library system, as represented by the catalog, received a given title in print was recorded regardless of the number of copies that may have been canceled. Since catalog records were relied on to denote holdings, any print item that was withdrawn from the collection after electronic access was enabled, that also had its catalog record deleted or suppressed from public view, could have been recorded inaccurately. In addition, it is possible that a library might have canceled the print version of a title before electronic access was made available, and this would not necessarily be apparent from catalog records.

There is also overlap among database coverage. In most instances, electronic versions were counted only if they were considered to be equivalent to the print version as noted in the *Gale Directory of Databases*. However, with *Biological Abstracts*, having access to either *Biological Abstracts* or *BIOSIS Previews* was considered acceptable for a library to be considered as having online access to the title.

The definition of what is considered a currently received title for the discussion on duplication is also problematic. Many of the ready reference titles are not published annually so a "current" version of the print title may not fall within the 2002-2003 time span that defines "current" for the purposes of this study. There are also some indexing and abstracting titles that have inconsistent publication cycles. For instance, *RILM Abstracts of Music Literature* released its 1998 print index in late February 2003. While the currency date was adjusted for this particular title, lesser delays in publication for other titles were not noted in the data. In addition, *Resources in Education: RIE* and *Current Index to Journals in Education: CIJE* ceased publication in 2001. These titles were excluded from the duplication discussion since it is impossible for a library to be currently duplicating the titles in both the print and electronic format.

DISCUSSION

Arts and Humanities

Looking at the data collected for the reference titles associated with the arts and humanities area, it is apparent that although anecdotal evidence would suggest those researching in this area are not apt to embrace technology and use it to meet their information needs, humanists are indeed using technology to find information–though whether this is by choice or by necessity is still not known. The majority of the indexing and abstracting titles for the arts and humanities area were duplicated in both print and electronic form by less than 40% of the libraries, with half of the titles being duplicated in multiple formats by less than 20% of the libraries. For the overall holdings of the arts and humanities titles, 90% of them are received online.

In an article about training humanists to use databases, Saule notes that "many humanists feel that scanning the printed *MLA International Bibliography* may, in fact, be easier than trying to outsmart the computer's terminology" and that "inexact humanistic language and discipline structures prevent controlled vocabulary searching from being entirely accurate" (604). Examining this statement from an article published in 1992 in the context of this study's findings would make one wonder if humanists still feel that their field is not adequately served with online databases. Of the libraries studied, only six (5%) are currently receiving *MLA International Bibliography* in print, and all of the libraries are receiving the title electronically. This suggests that humanists are: (1) no longer relying on *MLA International Bibliography* to find information, (2) sorely disappointed with the libraries' ability to meet their needs for finding information, or (3) have learned to adapt to the new technologies after all.

In her 1995 article, "A Brave New World: User Studies in the Humanities Enter the Electronic Age," Reynolds discusses the information gathering habits of humanists and how the traditional habits translate into the era of electronic information. She states that humanists:

> work alone, do not delegate research, sometimes rely on browsing, use books and older material, use mainly monographs, rely heavily on their own personal collections, value libraries, use a wide variety of material rather than a well-defined core of material, cite unique items located in special collections and often do not like using microforms. (62-63)

It is suggested that searching in the humanities may be more complex than searching in the sciences, due to the lack of a systematic language. One advantage of online resources over print for humanists may be the ability to use natural language to combine search terms (keyword searching), rather than having to rely on imperfect terms used in a controlled vocabulary (67). Since humanists rely heavily on books and special collections for their research, they may not be as reliant on indexing and abstracting resources as other disciplines. This may be why libraries do not maintain print access to titles available electronically, even when the discipline as a whole is portrayed in the literature as being print reliant and hesitant to embrace technology.

Social Sciences

The trends in the last print issue received for the social sciences closely mimic those of the arts and humanities titles. The majority of the indexing and abstracting titles for the social sciences area were duplicated in both print and electronic form by less than 40% of the libraries. When including *Resources in Education: RIE* and *Current Index to Journals in Education: CIJE* in the duplication data, the majority of the social sciences indexing and abstracting titles are being duplicated by less that 15% of the libraries studied. Overall, 92% of the holdings for titles in the area of social science are online. If considering only the indexing and abstracting titles, this number jumps to 97% of the holdings available online.

In "Information Seeking Patterns: Social Sciences," Folster reviews three decades of studies on how social scientists acquire information to meet their research needs. From these studies, she concludes:

> (1) Social scientists place a high amount of importance on jour-nals; (2) Most of their citation identification comes from journals, a practice that has been referred to as 'citation tracking'; (3) Infor-mal channels, such as consulting colleagues and attending confer-ences, are an important source of information; and (4) Library resources, such as catalogs, indexes, and librarians, are not very heavily utilized. (90)

Based on Folster's findings, it is not surprising that such a large percent-age of the social sciences indexing and abstracting titles that were ex-amined were purchased in the online format. Since social scientists place importance on journal literature, it seems logical that anything that would expedite finding such information would be readily accepted by them. Folster claims that social scientists do not use library re-sources, but the usage of the titles purchased is beyond the scope of this paper. However, it is implausible that libraries would maintain sub-scriptions to titles not utilized by the field, and usage statistics for elec-tronic resources are much more readily available than they are for their print counterparts.

Sciences

Findings in the sciences are surprising. Common sense says that sci-entists would be early adopters of the technology they helped create and would be willing to cast aside the print versions of titles to more fully embrace the functionality technology provides. However, this study paints a slightly different picture of scientists. Of all the titles and librar-ies studied, only 81% of the holdings are online in the area of the sci-ences. When looking at the data for indexing and abstracting titles for the sciences alone, this number does rise to 90%, but this is still some-what lower than the percentage of holdings online for the same types of resources in the social sciences and is the same as that of the arts and hu-manities. The sciences also had two (20%) of the indexing and abstract-ing titles examined being duplicated in print and electronic formats by over 50% of the libraries studied; however, half of the indexing and ab-stracting titles examined in the sciences are duplicated by only 20% of the libraries studied.

In "Scientists, Information Seeking, and Reference Services," Von Seggern considers how scientists use libraries and information. Von Seggern reports that scientists do not traditionally rely on library collections to meet their information needs nor do they require the assistance of librarians to find needed information (96). She notes creativity, individualistic tendencies, and time constraints as the reasons scientists bypass the library (99). Scientists rely heavily on refereed journals to disseminate information, but "[p]hysical accessibility appears to be an important factor in the determination of what is read and cited by researchers" (97-98). Since physical accessibility is noted as an important factor in whether or not scientists use information, it would seem that there would be an even higher percentage of the resources studied available online. Online access would mean that scientists could access the information from their homes or from their labs.

Concerns for Moving to Primarily Electronic Holdings

Although *The New York Times Index* was excluded from the overall analysis of the data, it is interesting to note that 93% of the institutions were still receiving it in print as of 2000, and 72% of the institutions received the print index in 2001. As a result of the Supreme Court decision in The *New York Times v. Tasini* case, electronic indexes are even more fluid than once thought, and the terms "comprehensive" and "full-text" in regard to electronic databases are now less meaningful than they once were.

In an article published in a January 2002 issue of *The Chronicle of Higher Education*, a spokesman for *The New York Times* noted that since the June 2001 Supreme Court ruling in favor of freelance authors "the newspaper has pulled 100,000 articles offline; however, 15,000 of those articles have since been restored after the paper struck deals with the writers." In the same article, a Gale spokesman is quoted as saying, "'We are making every attempt to retain citation indexing and written abstracts whenever possible.' If the abstract was written by the author however, it has to go, and Gale doesn't put anything in its place" (Carlson, "Once Trustworthy"). In a provider's haste to comply with the Supreme Court decision in the Tasini case, it is possible that entire entries for records of articles written by freelance writers were removed. If this were the case, without a print back-up, libraries would lose indexing to a large number of articles.

CONCLUSION

The trend among academic ARL libraries is to cease receiving print versions of titles in lieu of electronic access. Though it is impossible to know with any certainty that libraries had electronic access before canceling the print, or simultaneously canceled the print when beginning their electronic access to the title, the evidence would suggest that libraries did indeed cease receiving print once they were comfortable with the electronic format of the title. The graphs presented indicate that print holdings were recorded as last being received in the mid- and late-nineties and that 2000 and 2001 showed even more titles last being received in print. The graphs show that duplication of titles in print and electronic formats is minimal for most titles and for most libraries.

Although this study has been useful for painting a picture of the current state of ARL institutions regarding the shift from print to electronic access of core reference titles, there are several other areas where further research should be done to add a little color to the picture. It is now known when libraries last received the print version of the core titles, but it is unknown why print versions ceased to be received. Budget restrictions or user preferences are two likely reasons, but a study surveying ARL libraries as to why they canceled print titles when they did and what criteria they used to make these decisions might be helpful for predicting future trends. It would also be beneficial to look at smaller non-ARL academic libraries and public libraries to see if the trends seen in this study are similar among different types of libraries.

SELECTED LIST OF WORKS CONSULTED

ARL Member Libraries. 6 March 2003. Association of Research Libraries. 7 April 2003 <http://www.arl.org/members.html>.

Hedblad, Alan, ed. *Gale Directory of Databases*. 2 vols. Detroit: Gale, 2003.

Katz, William A. *Introduction to Reference Work: Volume I, Basic Information Sources*. 7th ed. New York: McGraw Hill Publishing Company, 1997.

REFERENCES

Carlson, Scott. "Once-Trustworthy Newspaper Databases Have Become Unreliable and Frustrating." *The Chronicle of Higher Education* 25 January 2002: 29. Online. Lexis Nexis Academic. 19 Mar. 2003 <http://www.lexis-nexis.com/universe>.

Davis, Trisha L. "The Evolution of Selection Activities for Electronic Resources." *Library Trends* 45.3 (1997): 391-403.

Folster, Mary B. "Information Seeking Patterns: Social Sciences." *The Reference Librarian* 49-50 (1995): 83-93.

Holleman, Curt. "Electronic Resources: Are Basic Criteria for the Selection of Materials Changing?" *Library Trends* 48.4 (2000): 694-710.

Kluegel, Kathleen. "The Reference Collection as Kaleidoscope." *RQ* 36.1 (1996): 9-11.

_____. "Revolutionary Times." *RQ* 35.4 (1996): 453-455.

Landesman, Margaret. "Sense & Sensibility–Multi-volume Reference Sets: Have They a Future?" *Against the Grain* 13.5 (2001): 82.

Okerson, Ann. "Are We There Yet? Online E-Resources Ten Years After." *Library Trends* 48.4 (2000): 671-693.

Palmer, Janet P. and Mark Sandler. "What Do Faculty Want?" *NetConnect* 128.1 (2003): 26-28.

Reynolds, Judy. "A Brave New World: User Studies in the Humanities Enter the Electronic Age." *The Reference Librarian* 49-50 (1995): 61-81.

Saule, Mara R. "User Instruction Issues for Databases in the Humanities." *Library Trends* 40.4 (1992): 596-613.

Schmitt, John. "Reference Purchasing: When Once Is Not Enough." *Against the Grain* 12.4 (2000): 24-26.

Von Seggern, Marilyn. "Scientists, Information Seeking, and Reference Services." *The Reference Librarian* 49-50 (1995): 95-104.

Wilkinson, Frances C. "Reference Materials–To Web or Not to Web? Librarians and Publishers Speak Out." *Against the Grain* 10.4 (1998): 1, 18-25.

_____. "Reference Materials–Where Formats and Budget Lines Collide: Librarians Speak Out!" *Against the Grain* 11.4 (1999): 1, 16-26.

APPENDIX

List of reference sources included in this study: Print title/Electronic title(s) if not the same as the print title, or the variant electronic title.

<u>General Resources</u>

Biography and Genealogy Master Index
Book Review Digest/Book Review Digest Plus
Book Review Index+
Books in Print*/Books in Print with Book Reviews
CQ Researcher*/CQ Library
Dissertation Abstracts/Digital Dissertations
The New York Times Index+
Readers' Guide to Periodical Literature/Readers' Guide Abstracts
Ulrich's Periodicals Directory*/Ulrichsweb

<u>Arts and Humanities Resources</u>

Art Index/Art Abstracts or Art Full Text
Arts & Humanities Citation Index/Web of Science
Grove Dictionary of Art+ *
MLA International Bibliography of Books and Articles on the Modern Languages and Literatures/MLA Bibliography
Music Index
New Grove Dictionary of Music and Musicians*
Philosopher's Index
RILM Abstracts of Music Literature

<u>Social Sciences Resources</u>

America: History and Life
Communication Abstracts+
Current Index to Journals in Education: CIJE/ERIC
Historical Abstracts: Bibliography of the World's Historical Literature/Historical Abstracts
Library Literature & Information Science
Mental Measurements Yearbook*
PAIS International in Print/PAIS International
Psychological Abstracts/PsycINFO
Resources in Education: RIE/ERIC
Social Sciences Citation Index/Web of Science
Sociological Abstracts/Sociofile

Sciences Resources

Bibliography and Index of Geology/GeoRef
Biological Abstracts/BIOSIS Previews
Chemical Abstracts/SciFinderScholar™
*CRC: Handbook of Chemistry and Physics**
Engineering Index/Compendex®/Engineering Village 2™ or Ei CompendexWeb
Index Medicus/MEDLINE or PubMed
Mathematical Reviews/MathSciNet
*McGraw-Hill Encyclopedia of Science & Technology**/AccessScience @
    McGraw-Hill: The McGraw-Hill Encyclopedia of Science and Technology
    on the Web!
Science Citation Index/Web of Science
Zoological Record

* Denotes titles that were excluded from discussions based on indexes and abstracts
  only.
+ Denotes titles that were examined in the original study but later excluded from the final analysis.

Revolution or Revelation?
Acquisitions for the Digital Library

Kathleen Morris
Betsy Larson

SUMMARY. Libraries are responding to customer preferences for electronic research materials through the acquisition and management of these products. Electronic resources have significantly different characteristics than print resources when it comes to technical services management. This paper addresses aspects of a corporate research library's evaluation of its collection development and maintenance practices as related to electronic materials: selection, contract negotiations, orders, cataloging, access management, and staff development. *[Article copies available for a fee from The Haworth Document Delivery Service: 1-800-HAWORTH. E-mail address: <docdelivery@haworthpress.com> Website: <http://www.HaworthPress.com> © 2006 by The Haworth Press, Inc. All rights reserved.]*

KEYWORDS. Negotiation, content selection, content access, staff development

---

Kathleen Morris is Manager, Library Services, Library Information Resources, Abbott Laboratories, Department 0441, Building AP6B, 100 Abbott Park Road, Abbott Park, IL 60064-6107 (E-mail: kathleen.morris@abbott.com). Betsy Larson is Library Systems Analyst, Library Information Resources, Abbott Laboratories, Department 043N, Building AP6B, 100 Abbott Park Road, Abbott Park, IL 60064-6107 (E-mail: betsy.larson@abbott.com).

[Haworth co-indexing entry note]: "Revolution or Revelation? Acquisitions for the Digital Library." Morris, Kathleen, and Betsy Larson. Co-published simultaneously in *The Acquisitions Librarian* (The Haworth Information Press, an imprint of The Haworth Press, Inc.) No. 35/36, 2006, pp. 97-105; and: *Integrating Print and Digital Resources in Library Collections* (ed: Audrey Fenner) The Haworth Information Press, an imprint of The Haworth Press, Inc., 2006, pp. 97-105. Single or multiple copies of this article are available for a fee from The Haworth Document Delivery Service [1-800-HAWORTH, 9:00 a.m. - 5:00 p.m. (EST). E-mail address: docdelivery@haworthpress.com].

Available online at http://www.haworthpress.com/web/AL
© 2006 by The Haworth Press, Inc. All rights reserved.
Digital Object Identifier: 10.1300/J101v18n35_07

CASE STUDY ENVIRONMENT

The Case Study library maintains a print collection of 8,000 monograph titles, 2,600 serial titles, and 1,300 active subscriptions. Additionally, the electronic collection consists of 700 active subscriptions and approximately 100 monograph titles. The library serves an international community of customers with diverse information requirements, including physical sciences, health care, information technology, competitive intelligence, and patents.

Acquisitions and cataloging processing for the print collections follows traditional practices within the environment of a local integrated library system application. Practices to record acquisitions data for electronic materials were originally defined in parallel with the library's practices for print materials; however, an additional separate Microsoft Access database was developed to maintain the extensive historical information for each electronic subscription. New practices may be required to support the activities and resulting wealth of data generated by the electronic content acquisitions process. As a result of expanding the acquisitions team responsibilities to include electronic published literature, the staff are actively evaluating acquisitions and cataloging processes for electronic monographs and subscriptions.

RESOURCE EVALUATION AND SELECTION

In pursuit of globalization efforts for the library's collections, electronic journals and books will necessarily replace some print resources within the collections. Decisions regarding which titles to maintain as print-only, electronic-only, or print-plus-electronic will be based upon criteria including customer focus group feedback, customer acceptance, ease of use, support for reference services, long-term relevance to the collection, collection space limitations, and per-use value of physical versus electronic access.

ELECTRONIC BOOKS

The future of e-books within the library has great potential. As described below, widespread customer acceptance of e-journals has sparked interest in electronic books. Customers actively recommend the library move the Information Technology (IT) and Science, Technology, and Medicine (STM) reference collections to electronic formats to improve accessibility and expand the collections.

Each electronic book vendor delivers a unique user interface. Search, display, and print functionality varies widely between vendor products. Each interface design has benefits and drawbacks, many of which are defined by local or personal preferences rather than product innovations or flaws.

ELECTRONIC JOURNALS

The library began acquiring access to electronic journals in 1998. Within the context of the library's corporate environment, the e-journal collection has expanded quickly and become extremely popular with customers.

Once a title selection is made, the next step to acquire access to the e-journal is identification of the most appropriate vendor. During the early years of e-journals, access was typically arranged though the current print-format aggregator or direct with the publisher. Access evaluation has evolved into a complex process, comparing such features as available file formats, print functionality, download/save options, archives availability, and pricing formulas.

The library's practical experience has shown that customers have a strong preference for PDF over HTML formatted documents. Color PDF documents and PDF with text indexing are increasingly requested. With the library's historical service emphasis on STM information, there is a significant requirement for historical archives of the journals, especially in the core physical sciences where these older resources continue to support business activities. In parallel with evaluating the availability of archive files is the forecasting for long-term viability of the access provider. E-journal title management becomes increasingly complex when access is maintained across multiple providers, each covering exclusive segments of the title.

CONTRACT AND LICENSE NEGOTIATIONS

The library's Digital Services team negotiates content contracts for the library, excluding e-journal negotiations. This team specializes in defining the company's diverse, global customer population and evaluating product usability. Electronic content products acquired for the library traditionally represented online research tools such as databases, news services, and full-text industry newsletters. Several desktop products recently implemented by the library's Digital Services team include collections of electronic textbooks. The majority of these e-books represent electronic versions of reference texts owned by the library in print format. Thus, the library's initial foray into e-books resulted from contracts for multi-format electronic information packages, with contracts negotiated outside the technical services team. Because of the origin of the contracts, traditional purchase order and vendor communications tracking has not been managed within the integrated library system. As the e-book collection is further developed and expanded the Technical Services and Digital Services teams will continue to work cooperatively to identify, evaluate, and implement e-books from a variety of aggregators. Tools for maintaining centralized information about contracts, purchase orders, and vendors are being developed by the library.

There is much opportunity for cooperation between library departments for the selection and implementation of e-books. These processes have traditionally been part of the Digital Services group responsibilities because of the fine line distinguishing e-books from online databases. To date all e-book acquisitions have resulted from direct customer title requests through database services. In the future, the library intends to expand e-book acquisitions to build a more robust collection.

Unlike print subscriptions management, no one source provides access to all or even the majority of e-journal titles the library seeks. The library staff needs to negotiate access rights and licensing with a complex combination of independent societies, small publishers, large publishers, and aggregators. The acquisition process is shifting from straightforward communications with a limited number of print subscription jobbers to a full negotiations sequence with multiple access providers with differing interpretations of access rights, licensing models and pricing formulas. The acquisitions team now maintains a wide variety of details related to e-journal subscriptions and is developing new skills in knowledge management.

During the first years of providing electronic content to end users, the contracts restricted customer access to those customers in the geographic region of the physical library campus. Access was further restricted through requirements for IP address ranges or ID/Password assignments. As the electronic collections grew in scope and popularity, and the library's intranet Web site became available to all company staff around the world, library staff recognized that managing local electronic collections was no longer appropriate. The library needed to provide global access to its resources for all knowledge workers in the company. Global licensing became a priority.

Negotiation of global, multi-site license agreements is a complex process. Vendors do not provide consistency or adhere to standards for access, pricing models or other license terms and conditions. Common examples of license models include: print plus an additional percentage for electronic delivery; multi-site or global surcharges; base content fee plus a percentage for print and/or electronic delivery; and cost calculated by total FTEs or knowledge workers (for corporate institutions). Additionally, vendors may utilize complicated formulas based on the total number of subscription copies across the institution to calculate the price for each print and electronic "copy." Other publishers may include a platform fee which can be "flat-fee" or based on the content value or based on FTEs.

The first step in the e-journal negotiation process is to interpret and understand the pricing model used by the vendor. It is important to appreciate not only the terms of access defined, but also the forms of access restrictions and cancellation penalties. Constraints imposed through the contract may include limitations on what titles the library will be permitted to cancel without penalties. Cancellation policies may also take the form of limitations based on a percent value of the prior year's total subscription cost; some publishers require libraries to maintain a minimum base subscription value defined by the previous year's subscription value, effectively preventing libraries from canceling titles without financial penalties.

Terms and conditions of license agreements vary widely. Library staff have necessarily become negotiators and interpreters of legal agreements for the acquisition of electronic content. Within the complex environment of license models and vendor-customer agreements, libraries and library communities are developing strategies to maximize their global information goals.

CATALOGING AND ACCESS

The library has made some policy decisions for the cataloging of e-books which may not comply with strict interpretation of cataloging standards. These decisions were made within the context of providing streamlined access to materials for customers. Cataloging of e-books where the library maintains a print version of the title involves creating a MARC 856 URL link within the print title's bibliographic record. The library has made the decision not to import secondary, format-specific MARC records for electronic titles, to reduce any potential confusion for customers. Cataloging of e-books where the library does not own a print version of the title involves local creation of a brief bibliographic record consisting of title, author, publisher, basic subject access, and URL links.

Once rights to a title are obtained, staff determine the best method of electronic access. Titles may be accessed directly at a publisher's Web site or through an aggregation vendor. Both forms of access present advantages and disadvantages. Aggregation vendors provide a gateway to the title content. The value of an aggregator's gateway is the common search, display, and print functionalities for a range of titles from multiple publishers, presented without embedded advertising. However, most aggregators do not provide proactive technical support. Technical problem resolution must be coordinated by the library staff: awareness, local troubleshooting, reporting to the aggregator, and communications with individual publisher support teams. The value of direct access from publishers is the absence of an intervening third-party vendor. If the library is able to obtain a large number of titles from a single vendor, then technical problem resolutions can be streamlined through a common communications venue. Unfortunately, each publisher Web site is unique, with no standards yet defined for these access tools. Training for customers requires extensive documentation to assist with accessing resources from multiple sources.

New tools are emerging in the library marketplace to address the complexities of access to large e-journal collections. These tools provide a single searching environment to identify e-journal titles available through library subscriptions with automatically maintained URL links. Additional product functionality may include table of contents files, links to document delivery services, and personalization portals.

STAFF DEVELOPMENT

As the nature of materials being processed evolves, so, too, does the nature of the work to acquire those materials. The basic processes of acquisitions remain, but many of the tools supporting these processes are changing: selection decisions, order and invoice management, and requester notification. Job descriptions and associated business skills must be transformed to accommodate the new library acquisitions environment.

Business processes are an integral element of the acquisitions staff knowledge base. Staff should possess a general understanding of how businesses operate for purchase orders, invoices, credit memos, samples delivery, and shipments. This general knowledge must then be integrated with a full understanding of the business environment of the library's selected content vendors.

Many library content vendors are providing Web-based systems for identifying inventory status, initiating orders, and tracking order progress. These ordering systems are augmenting or replacing the use of acquisitions functionality within libraries' integrated library system applications. Libraries may be shifting their order maintenance processes to the vendors' systems for all or some of their acquisitions. The libraries then need to decide whether to pursue options to import the bibliographic, order and/or invoice data into their local ILS. Staff need to develop and maintain their skills to utilize Web-based applications and manipulate data with tools such as MS Excel. If data is going to be exported from an external vendor system and imported into the local integrated library system, then staff also need to develop the necessary export/import and troubleshooting skills.

Electronic Data Interchange (EDI) technology has grown in popularity during recent years. More libraries are exchanging purchase order, claims, and invoice data with their vendors through EDI functionality provided by their ILS. While basic EDI transactions are not complicated to complete, the necessary ILS systems configuration requires a solid knowledge of the ILS product. Troubleshooting EDI errors necessitates a thorough understanding of the data being exchanged and all systems involved with the exchange.

Given these evolving environments for acquisitions records, acquisitions staff members need to continuously develop their technology skills and general business systems knowledge.

ACCOUNTABILITY

Copyright awareness in the days of print-only materials primarily required posting copyright notices by photocopiers. The ease of downloading and forwarding content electronically has made increased awareness and training of customers in the area of copyright a requirement. The library has developed an Intranet Web site with copyright

FAQs, a basic copyright brochure, and links to external copyright resources. An institutional team has been established and is led by the library to market copyright compliance standards for the organization.

In the traditional print library, vendors typically included a book jobber, a serials subscription agent, and a limited number of independent publishers. A digital library utilizes a wider variety of vendors and service providers to deliver content to customers. Titles may be sourced from the originating publisher as well as other service providers, depending on format preferences and accessibility requirements. This potential for using multiple vendors to obtain information content allows for selecting the best products for the customers and environment, but imposes complexities for financial tracking and reporting.

The library has a fresh opportunity to coordinate information content purchases throughout the organization. A coordinated approach to this process can result in maximizing purchasing power. Through educated and coordinated communications throughout the organization and with vendors, the library can facilitate information content access for the best value to the organization.

Financial accountability encompasses a change from utilizing a limited number of vendors to support a print collection to an extensive number of diverse vendors to support a print-plus-digital collection. This shift presents the library with opportunities to more effectively position itself within the larger organization's purchasing environment. The organization can then move from a distributed information content purchasing model to a cooperative, streamlined strategy for acquiring information products.

CONCLUSIONS

As the library progresses with its electronic collections strategy, services and staff responsibilities evolve dramatically. Library staff experience revelations around opportunities for interdepartmental purchasing power, copyright awareness and global knowledge exchange. Revolutions are occurring throughout contract negotiations, content provider service expectations, and staff skills development. Exciting times are ahead for the acquisitions team, especially contrasted with the now rose-colored rear view mirror perspective of print-only collection management.

REFERENCES

Berin, Andrew. "Unbundled Journals: Trying to Predict the Future." *Learned Publishing* 15.2 (2002): 109-112.

Bluh, Pamela, Marc Truitt, and Bob Boissy. "Serials Systems: Present and Future Considerations." *Serials Review* 28.2 (2002): 93-101.

Breeding, Marshall. "Offering Remote Access to Restricted Resources." *Information Today* 18.5 (2001): 52-53.

Christou, Corilee, and Gail Dykstra. "Through a 'Content Looking Glass'–Another Way of Looking at Library Licensing of Electronic Content." *Against the Grain* 14.5 (2002): 18, 20, 22.

Levack, Kinley. "Books 24x7: All of the Info All of the Time." *EContent* 26.2 (2003): 52-53.

Heimer, Gail L. "Defining Electronic Librarianship: A Content Analysis of Job Advertisements." *Public Services Quarterly* 1.1 (2002): 27-43.

Jordan, Mark, and Dave Kisly. "How Does Your Library Handle Electronic Serials? A General Survey." *Serials* 15.1 (2002): 41-46.

Montgomery, Carol Hansen, and JoAnne L. Sparks. "The Transition to an Electronic Journal Collection: Managing the Organizational Changes." *Serials Review* 26.3 (2000): 4-18.

Satin, Seymour. "Negotiating: From First Contact to Final Contract." *Information Today* 9.6 (2001). 4 April 2003 <http://www.infotoday.com/searcher/jun01/satin.htm>.

Watson, Paula D., ed. *E-journal Management: Acquisition and Control*. Spec. issue of *Library Technology Reports* 39.2 (2003): 1-80.

Wiegand, Sue. "Incorporating Electronic Products into the Acquisitions Workflow in a Small College Library." *Library Collections, Acquisitions, and Technical Services* (2002): 363-366.

The Decline of Print:
Ten Years of Print Serial Use
in a Small Academic Medical Library

Karen Thompson Rosati

SUMMARY. Tracking use of print journals over a ten-year period has allowed The University of South Carolina (USC) School of Medicine Library an essential tool for more accurate collection development, for both print and electronic selection. This lengthy study has provided usage statistics for purchasing decisions regarding electronic subscriptions still relevant to the present time. Total collection print journal use studies, never numerous in the library literature, may lose their validity as print use continues to fall. By the end of 2002, The USC School of Medicine Library's print journal use had fallen 85% from 1992 levels, including usage drops in both titles with and without electronic counterparts. The removal of print journals during a renovation is conjectured to have speeded patron use of e-journals. Based on the precipitous decline of print journal use, all library procedures are being examined closely for needed changes. [Article copies available for a fee from The Haworth Document Delivery Service: 1-800-HAWORTH. E-mail address: <docdelivery@haworthpress.com> Website: <http://www.HaworthPress.com> © 2006 by The Haworth Press, Inc. All rights reserved.]

Karen Thompson Rosati is Head of Serials, The University of South Carolina School of Medicine Library, USC, Columbia, SC 29208 (E-mail: Krosati@med.sc.edu).

[Haworth co-indexing entry note]: "The Decline of Print: Ten Years of Print Serial Use in a Small Academic Medical Library." Rosati, Karen Thompson. Co-published simultaneously in *The Acquisitions Librarian* (The Haworth Information Press, an imprint of The Haworth Press, Inc.) No. 35/36, 2006, pp. 107-117; and: *Integrating Print and Digital Resources in Library Collections* (ed: Audrey Fenner) The Haworth Information Press, an imprint of The Haworth Press, Inc., 2006, pp. 107-117. Single or multiple copies of this article are available for a fee from The Haworth Document Delivery Service [1-800-HAWORTH, 9:00 a.m. - 5:00 p.m. (EST). E-mail address: docdelivery@haworthpress.com].

Available online at http://www.haworthpress.com/web/AL
© 2006 by The Haworth Press, Inc. All rights reserved.

Digital Object Identifier: 10.1300/J101v18n35_08

KEYWORDS. Electronic journals, print usage decline, percentage statistics

INTRODUCTION

In the past three or more years academic medical libraries have experienced an overwhelming increase in the use of electronic journals and the declining use of print journals held in their collections. The USC School of Medicine Library in Columbia, South Carolina is no exception. However, this transition is somewhat unique in that since 1992 there has been an ongoing collection of detailed use statistics for all print serials. Most libraries have never institutionalized a daily routine where all uses of print journals are captured by title. Keeping statistics for ten years of use of print journals has allowed statistical analysis of current subscriptions for collection development of print and electronic resources. These statistics show in detail the profound decline in the use of all print serials.

Based on current usage statistics for both print and online, The USC School of Medicine Library's data show the percentage of print use decline in all journals, including those that have no online counterparts. The more than 80% drop of use over a ten-year period, subsequent to online access, indicates a major change in the usefulness of print journal statistics, in addition to heralding the overwhelming use of electronic journals. Are print journals an artifact of the past? And consequently, are print usage studies also headed for the dustbin? According to the statistics gathered by the School of Medicine Library, a few last looks at the print data will most likely have a number of useful points to impart, but serial print studies, never numerous, are approaching their end stages due to extremely low print journal use.

The University of South Carolina School of Medicine Library serves a small medical school, with less than 600 total students including doctoral and master's candidates. Current serial subscriptions number under 900, down from a high of 1,300 in 1983. The library is part of the larger University of South Carolina Columbia campus, and is currently able to access many databases and journals the School of Medicine Library itself does not subscribe to.

Why did the library commit to an ongoing print usage study? The advanced nature of the library's first online catalog (the now defunct Library Information System [LIS] from Georgetown University designed specifically for medical libraries) and the manageable collection size made it possible to collect use statistics for all library journal titles. The decision to barcode all issues and collect statistics was made in early 1992. There was an additional expense to barcode every issue received in the library, but this cost was small compared to the value of the data obtained and the convenience for patron check-out, as journals (except most recent issues) circulated.

Journal subscriptions had been cut on a regular basis since 1985 and without use data, decisions were made haphazardly. The tracking of all internal journal uses aided in making informed cancellation decisions based primarily on cost per use. Deciding to collect internal journal usage on a daily basis was only slightly controversial. When first faced with integrating this task into the daily routine, there was a concern that it would be too time consuming. Serials staff responsible for check-in agreed to gather and wand all of the information initially to determine what kind of workload was involved. Journals that were to be shelved were taken by truckload to the serials department for data collection before shelving. All journals reshelved had their barcodes wanded into the serials module as internal use. Circulation statistics were maintained separately from internal use. Internal use statistics were by title and included internal use of journals, as well as circulated use. Signs were put up all over the library informing patrons that they should not re-shelve any journals as a journal use study was in progress.

It became apparent early on to the student workers that it was the actual shelving that took the most time, not data collection. Soon there was general enthusiasm for the process. The work was done at a computer with a barcode reader, on both floors of the library. In a few weeks all usage was being captured. Collecting the data became even easier when barcodes were added to the spines of the 60,000 bound journals, for quicker circulation and inventory. At the end of each year, use statistics were added to a copy of our vendor's invoice beside each title. In the early years, this cumulated copy was checked regularly for titles with low use when cancellations were necessary.

The validity of collected usage by title was verified in 1998 when a substantial journal cancellation project, necessitated by a flat budget, was implemented. Fifty-one journals totaling $80,000, or 20% of the serial budget, had only 3% of total use. By offering interlibrary loans free to patrons for articles from cancelled journals, it was felt that this would identify journals patrons still wanted. (A flat per article charge of $4.00 has been in place for over 10 years for all patrons.) Notices announcing free articles were posted on current issues as well as back volume shelving for each title. At the end of one year, there had been less than 20 articles requested from the cancelled journals.

From 1996 to the present an additional important use of print journal statistics was to justify the purchase of electronic access for titles showing high use for current subscriptions. A concerted effort was made to provide and purchase online access to the 100 most used journals. If available, online versions of these journals were purchased from OVID, or later were purchased for additional fees from publishers if our print did not come with the online version. With the purchasing of online access to our most used journal titles, patrons were first introduced to online journals by being able to use electronic versions of titles they had already used extensively in print.

In 2000 there was a migration to a new integrated library system, Innovative Interfaces, as the LIS system was no longer being supported. This change split up usage data for the year, but an improved internal use module could provide internal usage statistics by not just title, but also volume, issue, and year. In 2001 print usage was once again somewhat unreliable as the library underwent a total renovation (May-September) of the second floor which held the majority of journals.

The renovation in 2001 necessitated that most print journals were unavailable to patrons for a five-month period, excepting titles which were identified as having no online versions at all. For these, four years of print was pulled and shelved downstairs in the monograph area. At that time, back-file use was the smaller portion of total print use, so four years was deemed to be far enough back to address most needs. Free interlibrary loans were offered to anyone needing articles, and since there was access to a number of e-journals by that time, patrons seemed only slightly inconvenienced by the print not being available. Interlibrary loan borrowing did double during a 3-month period, but was not as heavy as anticipated.

Looking back at the decline in print use after the renovation was completed, it was easy to conjecture that patrons got a head start on using e-journals out of necessity. This also encouraged staff to direct patrons to online journals, which may have been another push in the electronic direction. Perhaps migration from print to electronic versions was inevitable, and renovation and more connected patrons happened independently of each other, but simultaneously. In any event, after the renovation, when our 70,000 journal volumes were back in place, the piles of print journals that needed to be re-shelved had become noticeably and measurably smaller.

Taking away the print seemed to have speeded the transition to electronic journals, as is shown in the recent 2002 University of California Collection Management Initiative. The study involved the removal of the print issues of a large group of titles, by discipline, which were available online, and the storage of those journals at a remote location, to be ordered from storage if necessary. The stored journals were the experimental group, and other journals were the control. Journals with print versions moved to storage showed practically no print use at all, and the electronic versions of the journals showed a quantum leap of use. Print use was a mere 201 for four quarters of 2002, and digital use extracted from publisher sites was 160,180. The control group, where print was still available, showed 6,044 print uses, and 97,493 electronic (http://www.ucop.edu/cmi/data_charts_usage.html). A natural conclusion is that when patrons are forced to break their habits of using print, and learn that the information they need is in electronic format and easily accessible, they drop the print gladly and run to the electronic.

Starting in 2002, the number of journals to reshelve, which had always been the bulk of reshelving in the library, was alarmingly small. Student workers who previously spent most of their time shelving were left with less to do. One student worker slot was cut, since by that time a 40-90% drop in the use of print journal titles, by title, could be documented by examining the list of most used journal titles on an Excel spreadsheet and noting the drop in print use.

From 1992-1996, the monthly total number of uses of print journals was approximately 3,000. As late as 1999, there were over 2,000 uses per month. At the end 2002, print use had declined to an average of 550 total uses per month. Taking the top 10 used journals in the 100 most used journals, and the bottom 10 in that list, the changes in print uses from their high to current day were almost identical: 85.4% and 85.2% respectively (see Table 1). Based on these almost identical declines in the print use of most used journals, and lesser used journals, the assumption is that all use of print has declined by this percentage.

With the amount of print use dropping so quickly, the analysis of print statistics demanded a different slant, such as which patrons were using the print and why? Are they unaware of online, is there online access we still need to purchase, how much use are back-files having? In looking for at least one answer: "Who is using the print?" the interlibrary loan technician began accounting month by month for how many print journals are used to fill interlibrary loans. Despite using e-journals as much as possible to fill loans to other libraries, statistics showed that by the second half of 2002, a monthly average of 150 (25%) of the print

TABLE 1. Decline of Print Use of Top Ten and Bottom Ten Most Used Journals

Rank	Title	1992-1999 High Prt use	2002 Prt use
1	*New England Journal of Medicine*	830	215
2	*JAMA*	653	164
3	*Science*	807	84
4	*Journal of Biological Chemistry*	566	33
5	*Nature*	672	69
6	*Proceeding of the National Academy of Sciences*	748	12
7	*Lancet*	476	89
8	*Cell*	506	32
9	*Annals of Internal Medicine*	280	93
10	*Circulation*	233	54
	Total print use	5771	845
	Total decrease in print use		85.4%
91	*Stroke*	94	45
92	*Thorax*	72	13
93	*American Journal of Human Genetics*	122	13
94	*Diabetes*	121	14
95	*American Heart Journal*	178	45
96	*Canadian Medical Association Journal*	69	6
97	*Clinical Chemistry*	71	8
98	*Experimental Cell Research*	93	9
99	*Journal of Urology*	134	20
100	*Journal of Cell Science*	123	1
	Total	1077	159
	Total decrease in print use		85.8%

journal use was accounted for by loans to other libraries, not patron use. The data run done from February 8-March 17, 2003 showed that print use was down to an average of 11 uses per day, or 341 per month. If this trend continues, annual use for 2003 will be approximately 4,100, or 40% lower than in 2002. More statistical analysis needs to be done to show what proportion of the print use is current versus backfile use, but a look at the first quarter of 2003 showed the data which follows in Table 2.

TABLE 2. Breakdown of Journal Use

Breakdown of use by journal year:

1999 and back = 210
2000-2001 = 57
2002 = 77
2003 = 69

Breakdown of use of 2000-2003 journals:

online access available = 162
online required usernames and password = 18
no online access = 36

An explanation for the further recent decline of print use is that in January 2003 the large full-text journal database KluwerOnline became available to our patrons, and consequently the drop in print use can likely be accounted for by continuing addition of electronic access. Previously there were only 12 of the Kluwer-Plenum titles in print available to our patrons. Currently we have online access to all 600+ Kluwer titles, 200+ of which are biomedically related.

There is conjecture among the staff that a number of the print uses are by users who are not primary patrons, such as local physicians or USC main campus students. Infrequent users may ask the library staff where the journals are shelved, and they are first directed to the print issues. At some point they would be directed to our e-journals page or catalog, but not if they found what they needed without help. Also, some physicians have remarked when asked for input about canceling print and going with online only, that it would be a shame to not have a current journal area where they can sit and read, indicating a continuing interest in browsing, at least in theory.

Although the primary topic of this article is the drop in print use and the implications for usage studies, there was of course a general awareness that electronic journals use was steadily increasing as print use was decreasing. Initially this change was difficult to measure as the first e-journal page was not set up to collect use statistics by title. Consequently, for a number of years, print statistics for collection development were used since electronic use statistics were not yet available for online titles, and only a few publisher sites were available which provided online use statistics.

By the beginning of 2001, as print use declined and electronic use increased, and to address changing needs, an internally designed e-journal database was created for our library by a USC database management group. E-journal information was manually input into a sequel database with the capability to track use by title. At the beginning of 2002, six months after the debut of the new e-journal page, there were 4,000 hits monthly. By January 2003, total hits were up to 10,000 per month, not including patron e-journal accesses that were through any other source than the e-journal page, such as PubMed.

Regarding the use of electronic statistics from publishers, the School of Medicine Library is affiliated with The University of South Carolina main campus in Columbia. As a small library we share the same range of IP addresses with the main campus, but medical school faculty members have their own discrete IP ranges, so most current publisher usage does not represent just medical school usage, but the entire University of South Carolina range of IPs. Consequently, most publisher usage data is not specific enough to aid School of Medicine collection development decisions, unless the publisher can provide IP range statistics. This is one reason that past print usage is still as valuable as it is in making decisions about which unit will pay for what title, especially if there is still subscription duplication.

In the case of our institution, using print journal statistics to purchase online access seemed to be very effective. Until a statewide agreement to provide ScienceDirect to academic libraries in 2001, there was no large publisher full-text database available to patrons, and all access was made available title by title as each became available electronically. As of 2002, all of the 100 most used titles were online and available to our patrons. By the end of 2002, 80% of the library's subscription titles were available online. The remaining 20% of these had impossible access restrictions, or very low previous print use and high cost for online, with the remainder not being available online at all. This 80% online, 20% not available statistic actually parallels the full text of journals available through PubMed. There are 4,600 titles indexed, and 3,750 or 83% now link to full text in that database which shows the broader picture of biomedical and clinical publications in transition.

Previous to 2002, print usage statistics were maintained on copies of our vendor invoices by title, with hardcopies of LIS reports kept for reference. We had meant to switch for a while from this low tech way of monitoring subscriptions. To get the big picture of change in electronic access, the serials department graduate assistant in 2002 began entering all current journals' past usage data into an Excel spreadsheet, with title, publisher, and ISSN. Electronic uses from the e-journal page were also added by title, and comparisons could be made between print and electronic use.

An indicator was added to the usage showing an "N" for titles without electronic access and results showed that all print use had declined. Print use had dropped to low levels for our most used titles, which was anticipated as all of these were available online in some format. However, the print use for titles with no electronic access available to our library also showed a 75% decline between 1999-2002 in the aggregate, as Table 3 shows. There were a very few titles without online access showing minimal or no decline in use.

Use of print journals without electronic access in the library may be dropping for a number of reasons. In a few cases, online access may be available to a personal subscriber, although if a patron had their own personal subscription to a title previously, they would have not been using the library's print copy. Additionally, tables of contents and abstracts of most journals are available online, even if the full-text is not. The library literature also stresses that patrons are willing to find information elsewhere if the online version of their first choice is not available. The larger picture is most likely a combination of all of the above.

CONCLUSION

Beginning in 2000, even before use of print journals had declined so drastically to current levels, it was decided that the few new print subscriptions ordered by the library must have electronic counterparts. This was based on patron affinity for using electronic versions that did not require them to come to the library to get their information. Since the renovation in 2001, the migration to electronic use by patrons has continued unabated. Any suggestion to a faculty member that they need to come to the library to see an article in a print journal is meet with incredulity. Some patrons working in the library who are told they cannot access a title online, but that it is available one floor up will decide that they would prefer not to bother. The decline of print use and the rise of electronic use changes drastically the way libraries are accustomed to doing business. Soon there may be little more to learn from the monitoring of print journal usage, other than that browsing of current journal is-

TABLE 3. Decline in Use of Print Journals with No Electronic Version Available

Title	2002	1999	1998	1997	1996	1995
Am J of Nursing	5	22	24	42	22	25
Am J of Orthopsychiatry	2	12	20	3	20	24
Am J of Tropical Medicine and Hygiene	0	20	25	19	37	28
Ann of Ophthalmology	0	2	7	14	23	25
Archives of Environmental Health	3	34	21	14	31	24
Aviat Space and Environ Med (abbr)	11	13	24	16	9	20
Behavioral Neuroscience	8	13	44	17	23	18
Clinical Pediatrics	1	31	22	37	42	30
Connecticut Medicine	10	43	30	33		
Digestive Diseases and Sciences	2	31	31	29	37	43
Electromyogr Clin Neurophysiol (abbr)	2	5	27	11	10	16
Genetic Counseling	10	23	12	18	27	25
Health Care Management Review	1	13	23	13	28	34
International J of Health Services	2	11	8	16	18	21
International Surgery	3	27	22	18	10	16
J of General Psychology	1	14	4	4	9	3
J of Speech, Lang Hear Res (abbr)	2	52	39	21	15	23
J of the Am Psychoanalytic Association	2	3	6	4	8	10
Metabolism: Clinical and Experimental	9	55	57	68	43	43
Military Medicine	18	23	57	30	49	41
Neuropediatrics	9	11	10	13	14	19
PC Magazine	21	37	29	75	120	83
Psychological Review	2	8	10	4	11	11
South African Medical J	8	25	40	25	30	28
Totals	133	528	592	544	636	610

sues is still in favor, or that some patrons do not like to use online journals that require usernames and passwords.

Based on the drastic drop in use and purchase of print journals outlined above, The USC School of Medicine Library is currently planning on discontinuing binding of journals. All procedures are now being examined for necessary changes. Even more print journals will be canceled with online only retained. Staff members are now taking on completely different tasks, and allocation of all resources will change accordingly. The print data collected over the last 10 years has been used in making a number of important decisions. And despite the low number of uses of print, it is planned that print usage monitoring will continue, with special attention to interlibrary loan, browsing, and back-file use. However, based on usage data, it is obvious that the most important aspects of journal use have shifted to the online. Print use statistics can still provide information for making decisions, but the preponderance of effort for statistical collection should now focus on electronic formats.

The Integrated Library System:
From Innovation to Relegation
to Innovation Again

Tracy Primich
Caroline Richardson

SUMMARY. The Integrated Library System remains a true innovation that forms the baseline of service provided by the contemporary library. The purpose of this paper is to take a moment and reflect upon this innovation, and also to comment about ways to boost and revive innovative endeavors that can further develop the ILS. *[Article copies available for a fee from The Haworth Document Delivery Service: 1-800-HAWORTH. E-mail address: <docdelivery@haworthpress.com> Website: <http://www.HaworthPress.com> © 2006 by The Haworth Press, Inc. All rights reserved.]*

Tracy Primich is Supervisor, RLIS (E-mail: tprimich@ford.com); and Caroline Richardson is Supervisor, Technical Services Unit, RLIS (E-mail: cricha20@ford.com), both at Ford Motor Company, PO Box 1602, Dearborn, MI 48121.

[Haworth co-indexing entry note]: "The Integrated Library System: From Innovation to Relegation to Innovation Again." Primich, Tracy, and Caroline Richardson. Co-published simultaneously in *The Acquisitions Librarian* (The Haworth Information Press, an imprint of The Haworth Press, Inc.) No. 35/36, 2006, pp. 119-133; and: *Integrating Print and Digital Resources in Library Collections* (ed: Audrey Fenner) The Haworth Information Press, an imprint of The Haworth Press, Inc., 2006, pp. 119-133. Single or multiple copies of this article are available for a fee from The Haworth Document Delivery Service [1-800-HAWORTH. 9:00 a.m. - 5:00 p.m. (EST). E-mail address: docdelivery@haworthpress.com].

Available online at http://www.haworthpress.com/web/AL
© 2006 by The Haworth Press, Inc. All rights reserved.
Digital Object Identifier: 10.1300/J101v18n35_09

KEYWORDS. Integrated library system, digital libraries, online catalogs

INTRODUCTION

The ILS is a good service. Pedestrian as it may seem, criticized as it is by the Nicholson Baker's of the world, unromantic as bits and bytes are when compared to beautiful oak cabinets, the Integrated Library System remains a true innovation that forms the baseline of service provided by the contemporary library. The purpose of this paper is to take a moment and reflect upon this innovation, and also to comment about ways to boost and revive innovative endeavors that can further develop the ILS.

First, though, we give an honest accounting of our biases. We are special librarians employed by a major corporation. Typical considerations for us include the following:

- A catalog that strictly adheres to the guidelines of AACR2 is an abstract concept. Our catalog and our cataloging practices are not things of beauty. We will never be rewarded by our parent company for having a model catalog. For us, function is everything.
- Each member of our staff must interact with the customer base in order to surprise and delight them. We do not have a staff whose exclusive purpose is to catalog. Our cataloging is outsourced so that on-site staff may deliver direct public service.
- Our performance is judged on how well we contribute to the bottom line of the company. We need to justify our existence on a continual basis by delivering essential information services. Our customers do not care about subject headings, but they do care about desktop delivery of information that makes them look good to their bosses.

We do not have the luxury of entertaining ideas or projects on cataloging per se. What we must do is use tools as efficiently and as flexibly as possible for the purpose of outstanding and innovative customer service. One of our most important tools is our ILS.

HISTORY OF THE ILS

The ILS, and its close relatives MARC and networking, have changed everything we do. Having processed overdues with McBee cards, we are eternally grateful for the ability to e-mail overdue notices (Williams 16). Consider the current inter-library system. A library patron can initiate an inter-library loan from a home institution's computer. The request is routed and tracked by the ILS and the patron gets what she wants with a process that seems, to her, transparent. For instance, in 1989 ILLINET Online celebrated its tenth birthday. During that ten-year period, patrons initiated nearly 2.5 million inter-library loan requests (Sloan 145). That is an inspirational number and one brought about by the deployment and use of networked systems and the MARC standard. The ILS is so common, so integrated into contemporary library practices, so ingrained in how we deliver the library's collections to the customer base, that we no longer notice what an innovation it was (see Table 1).

TABLE 1. Brief History of the ILS and MARC

1963	Florida Atlantic University buys an IBM mainframe (4K of memory!!) with the intent of building a library management system, including a book catalog. The project made a big splash in the literature, but the system never became fully operational.
1963	LC creates the Office of the Information Systems Specialist. The Big Idea is to create a resource for pooling and distributing computerized records.
1965	Staff at LC is in place and working on the creation of a standardized format for record input.
1967	OCLC (then called Ohio College Library Center) was established for the purpose of building a database of MARC records.
1970	ANSI's Subcommittee on Machine Input Records approved MARC II as a national standard.
1971	OCLC is online and operational.
1978	Research Libraries Group is formed and RLIN (Research Libraries Information) is created and so is another source of MARC records.
1981	OCLC changes its name to reflect its de facto national status. It is now called Online Computer Library Center.
1986	A survey of ARL (Association of Research Libraries) members reveals that most member institutions were either planning or had completed retrospective conversion cataloging projects.
1990	While homegrown systems were implemented in the early days of ILSs, by 1990 turnkey systems are standard purchases.
1990	OCLC staff had converted 48 million bibliographic records, using the national standard of MARC.
Early 1990s	Catalogs are frequently augmented by mounting databases on the catalog architecture.

(Milsap 79; Spicher 75)

WITHOUT A CATALOG,
A LIBRARY IS JUST A PILE OF BOOKS

We used this sentence to explain quickly, crudely, but effectively to management why we needed an online library system. Its existence is a core service and maintaining the ILS is a core competency of our profession. Joseph Matthews (Matthews 1) says, "The creation of a library's catalog is a process that adds value to the information." He points out three processes identified by R. S. Taylor that add value to information: "organizing, analyzing, judgmental." This is what librarians do when we add information to an ILS. We organize, we analyze, and we make judgments about what content to include and how to describe that content in the metadata we wrap around the content. The principles that librarians use to add value to content, information, books–whatever we want to call it–have not changed in hundreds of years. Card catalog, or OPAC or WWW, the process of organizing, analyzing, and judgment are the same. The tools change and how both librarians and library users interact with those tools change, but the principles are the same whether the content is leather manuscripts or electronic images of those same manuscripts.

WHY THE ILS STILL MATTERS

Libraries Spend a Great Deal of Money on Them

Libraries have a great deal invested in the ILS. The gross revenue for automated library systems sales and services in 2001 was estimated to be $530 million. That is up 17% from the year before (Breeding 48). Since many institutions do not purchase or lease their hardware from library vendors, this number is undoubtedly under representative of the year's direct expenditures by libraries for automation systems and services. The direct dollar expenditure for automation is a very big number.

Libraries Devote Significant Staff Time to Them

Preparation of RFPs, evaluating responses, and then implementing a new system is a major effort for any library staff. Keeping up with software upgrades, equipment maintenance, and general system maintenance, such as regular backups and regular monitoring of the system, are ongoing staffing requirements. The people who usually do this work tend to be some of the most highly paid staff. In the *Library Journal* 2001 annual Placements and Salaries Survey, (with the exception of one lucky Webmaster at $55,000) the highest average salary for beginning librarians was for automations/systems positions at $43,731 (Terrell 30).

The staffing costs do not stop with the people directly responsible for the system. Since almost every task done by the library staff is done on the system, there are initial and ongoing staff training costs with each system change and upgrade. Each enhancement to the circulation module requires some new training for the circulation clerks. The software vendor's move to provide new features for MARC holdings statements may require the serials staff to revamp their procedures. Addition of EDI capability may enable more efficient ordering of materials. All these events require analysis time for supervisory staff and training time for everyone. All of this effort represents cost in staff time.

The ILS Includes All of the Libraries' Holdings, Representing a Huge Investment of Cataloging Effort

For decades libraries have been adding records to their Integrated Library Systems. One study found cataloging cost ranging from $12.22 for the copy cataloging of a monograph to $88.24 for cataloging a serial, with an overall average cost per record of $16.25 (Morris 44). And remember retro conversion projects? With great persistence and much cooperative sharing of cataloging data, libraries converted their cards to electronic records for their entire collections. Our legacy data is now for the most part in the same format as our current data.

MARC Format Is Excellent Metadata

MARC format coupled with AACR2 (*Anglo American Cataloging Rules*, 2nd ed., and ISBD (*International Standards for Bibliographic Description*) have worked very well for librarians. MARC has given us a common record, and standards have provided the discipline required to create consistent records. The economic necessity of sharing cataloging data and the genius of MARC have combined to give us a tremendous body of consistent metadata describing the intellectual content of centuries of human experience.

MARC vs. XML

There has been criticism of MARC and insistence in some quarters that we must abandon this data form originally created to produce catalog cards back in the 1960s. Certainly the argument is that a data format, such as XML, that is consistent with data in the rest of the information technology universe and the Web would allow for the use of programming suites developed for non-library purposes. This could possibly provide more options for system vendors and more options for local library customization, as programming would not have to deal with the unique characteristics of MARC. However, we have over 30 years of experience with MARC during which time we have learned, modified, figured out how to make it work for a very large number of different kinds of content.

In 1996 the Ford Research Library converted from our original non-MARC system to a SIRSI Unicorn system. One of our biggest concerns was that we were converting to MARC records. We had already outsourced our cataloging and no one on the staff was particularly MARC literate or much inclined to become so. We must admit MARC was pretty much thought of as "that bun-head" library system. Reference snobs that we were, none of us wanted to delve into the difference between a 245 and a 246 tag or be able to explain what a fixed field was. After a steep learning curve, we have become most impressed with the power of MARC and the ability of library systems to manipulate it. We have been able to find appropriate MARC tags to describe any content we have wanted to add to our database and been able to use the nuances of sub-fields and indicators to display or not display, index or not index a variety of elements. We electronically load a variety of non-traditional content including Society of Automotive Engineers technical papers, in-house electronic research reports, and articles from our in-house electronic technical journal.

In the many years librarians have worked with MARC the standard has been expanded and adapted for new formats and types of content. There is no other metadata schema with this kind of real world use with real documents. While MARC has its faults, it has allowed us to build the library automation system and shared cataloging infrastructure we have enjoyed for many years. As we work to meet the challenges of the future, we need to be careful not to throw out the baby with the bath. As put clearly by Alan Danskin, "any replacement for MARC has to offer a 'killer application' which would justify replacing the infrastructure in which we have invested so much" (Danskin 2).

ENTER, THE WEB

The year 1995 is one we remember well because it was the year that the library at Ford Motor Company launched its first Web site. It was an exciting event for us. Our open house that year, with the homepage as the guest of honor, was standing room only, and the madding crowd devoured the enormous sheet cake in twenty minutes. The ILS, in place and successfully used around Ford for a decade, was about to be eclipsed by the new acronym, WWW. Although CD-ROM was the interesting technology in the mid-1980s, and gophers were state-of-art in the early 1990s, by the late 1990s, Web servers were de rigueur in libraries. By the late 1990s, indexing and abstracting services had moved to Web delivery of service. If a library was upgrading its ILS turnkey software, it needed a Web interface.

In terms of budget and razzle-dazzle, Web resources command the attention of library staff and library customers. In general, the ILS is not used as the platform for these resources, and the ILS is now "a" resource instead of "the" resource. A small example: The University of Texas reported in 2001 that 15% of its funds were expended on electronic information (University of Texas at Austin, "Books, Journals, and Electronic Resources"). As is now typical for libraries, the University of Texas library Web site is the main entry point for the delivery of services, with navigation to a variety of electronic resources. UTNetCat, the University of Texas' OPAC, is one of many resources on the homepage, and, from a graphical and design perspective, is no more or less prominently displayed than a variety of other resources. Even in the current times of dot bomb, programmers earn more than librarians (Jacobs 284). Resource development and resource dollars are increasingly framed in terms of digital (i.e., Web) libraries.

DIGITAL LIBRARIES ARE KEY

We are not at all unnerved or defensive about the development of digital libraries, the availability of Web-based interfaces to indexing services, or the dramatic shift in the budget to support digital purchases over traditional ones. Which would we rather use: *Science Citation Index* or Web of Science? Printed *Chemical Abstracts* or SciFinder? The *Official Gazette* or MicroPatent? Digital versions are usually preferable, to staff and to library customers.

Our concern is that with concentration centered on the development of ever better Web pages, the ILS may become a poor relation. It is of concern to us that the catalog often does not do what we want it to do. It is of concern to us that innovation with the catalog involves a concentrated, multi-year effort of training in proprietary software, of being an outspoken and long-term advocate with the vendor, and of being a coordinator of efforts between vendors.

WISHES FOR INCREASED FUNCTIONALITY FOR THE ILS

We have engaged in a number of innovative projects with our Integrated Library System. We would have preferred to use standard utilities or reports to accomplish these tasks, but this was not possible with our current ILS. Our examples are all custom jobs that need to be maintained (sigh) with each upgrade.

Wish for Metadata Transparency and Metadata Mapping Tools: Example of SAE and Proprietary Reports

The Society of Automotive Engineers Technical Reports is a literature that is core to our library. Approximately 3,000 SAE records per year are added to the OPAC, and they must be added as soon as they are published by SAE. In addition to electronic pdf files of the papers, which we mount internally, we receive a flat ASCII file of bibliographic records for each batch of papers. We mapped SAE's metadata to appropriate MARC tags and use the standard bibliographic load report to load the data into our catalog complete with a URL link to the full report.

In a similar fashion we load author-supplied metadata for Ford research reports and the *Ford Technical Journal* (FTJ) into the OPAC. As part of the publication process, scripts harvest the metadata from these publications in order to create a file of bibliographic records that also contain links to the full-text. The metadata is mapped to the appropriate MARC tag, and the file is loaded into the catalog.

Because the value of good authority control is totally unappreciated in our corporate environment, for both SAE and our internal metadata we have mapped subject fields as a MARC index term (653 tag), which is not under authority control but indexed in the subject keyword index. This allows us to keep subject authority on data loaded from normal bibliographic sources. Corporate affiliation is also an authority problem. This information is often important to our users when searching the SAE technical papers, but SAE includes it exactly as listed by the authors, so there are more variations on the names of major automotive manufacturers and suppliers than imaginable. We mapped this information to the affiliation subfield of the MARC personal name (100 subfield u) and indexed it in the author keyword index. This allows us to keep some authority control over corporate author for other materials. While our cavalier liberties with authority control may be appalling to more traditional catalogers, these automated processes allow us to add mission-critical, non-traditional data to our catalog quickly and with very little cost per record.

Wish for Streamlined Acquisitions

One innovation we attempted but ultimately abandoned was an effort to streamline our acquisitions process. As in most libraries, our professional staff shares collection development responsibilities. We wanted to find a way for our selectors to search a book jobber's database via the Web, choose what they wanted and order it on the vendor's site, and have the vendor send us a MARC bibliographic record with our order attached ready for loading into our systems. We worked with Blackwell when its Collection Manager system was first introduced in order to implement such an arrangement. While we were able to place the order online, and Blackwell was able to send us bibliographic records, once those records where loaded into the database, our clerical staff had to go into our system and create the order. There was no way to load the bibliographic information and the order in one step. We are chronically short of clerical staff so the major impetus for the project was to get the computers to complete the clerical tasks once the selector had authorized the purchase and designated the funding and holdings location. Since we still had to have clerical staff create the order on our system, what we were able to come up with at the time was not any more efficient than loading OCLC records and manually creating an order. Currently most efforts in using electronic orders has been directed to using EDI in order to send orders from a local system to the vendor. We would like the to see the process the other way around, and make use of the vendor's Web site to generate the order simultaneously with the vendor and within our ILS.

Wish for Easy Processing of Grey Literature: Example of the Conference Board

The Conference Board is an independent, membership organization that engages in research and forecasting activities that pertain to business issues and business strategies. The Conference Board publishes a highly regarded series of analyses and research reports. Ford Motor Company is a member of the Conference Board, and members are entitled to copies of the reports. The Conference Board is able to provide bibliographic data but not in MARC format or in any kind of traditional metadata. Bibliographic data was supplied on an Excel spreadsheet. While we wanted the records in the catalog, we did not want to do original cataloging for each report. A summer intern programmed an Access database that imported tagged data, comma delimited data, or spreadsheets, and converted the data to MARC format, including an 856 tag. With the PDF version of the Conference Board report loaded onto our server, users could search the catalog and display Conference Board reports.

Wish for Security Protocols That Are Transparent to the User: Example of Automated Login

Another successful innovation is the use of Ford's corporate supported network login system, known in Ford parlance as "Web Single Login" or WSL, to identify users when they click on the online catalog. Users need know only their WSL password, and they remain oblivious to what their PIN (personal identification number) is for logging into the OPAC. Employees login once with WSL, and authentication is carried from one site. When a user comes to our online catalog, the system checks to see if they a registered library user. If so, the system queries our database for the user's PIN, supplies it, and logs the user into the catalog as him or herself. In addition to allowing the user to see their own library account including their checkouts and holds, this also invokes two other SIRSI features, accountability and choice of language to view the catalog. Accountability allows us to prevent un-authorized users from having access to company proprietary information contained in the database. Since we have users all over the world, the language choice allows users to search the catalog in their own language. We currently support Spanish and German in addition to English.

We have also used the corporate LDAP server to allow users to register themselves for library services and to keep our user database up-to-date. LDAP is automatically queried for the user address, phone, employment category, etc. Once the user confirms this information is correct, he submits the registration and his information goes into a file that is batch loaded into our ILS once an hour. Once per week, we run a program that matches all library users against LDAP, updates any changed information, deletes users no longer with the company, and alerts library staff to users who are no longer in LDAP but may have holds or materials checked out, allowing us to take appropriate action.

Wish for Flexible Searching: Example of One Search

As is common on library Web sites, the RLIS homepage has a search function for querying all the resources available on the site. Search logs clearly demonstrate that users of the library Web site expect to find item level material as a result of entering a statement into the search box. We wanted to query the catalog from the general library search box and frame the search results by using the environment of the library Web site, rather than displaying results strictly from within the interface of the online catalog. This proved to be a challenge. We are blessed with a skilled programming staff, and they developed methods that used Perl to mimic a user and overcome security concerns. Although our system comes equipped with the ability to query the database from a command line, the commands did not provide the kind of flexibility that we required.

Wish for More Collection Management Tools: Example of E-Journals

Like all libraries, we struggle to manage our e-journals. They are purchased from a variety of sources, and knowing which titles are available electronically, and which volumes are available electronically, are common questions from our customers. Those who predict the obsolescence of libraries, never talked to a serials librarian. To put it bluntly, other than an 856 field, our ILS does not offer much assistance in coping with the problem of managing e-journals. However, it is possible to purchase services that manage collection of electronic serials. These services include Serials Solutions, Journal Web Cite, and TDNet. EBSCO has recently entered this arena with its Electronic Journals Service. You can buy MARC records, create A-Z lists of content, and track licenses. While content providers clearly play a role in providing services for the management of e-journals, we would welcome more activity in this area on the part of ILS developers. The online catalog is, after all, a database. Strategic partnering with existing developers of e-journal management software can make sense, and use of the existing ILS software can be extended.

NOT JUST A CLICHE: THE FUTURE IS NOW

An exhaustive survey of the literature reveals that there are many interesting research projects currently underway, the results of which may make their way into next generation ILS products. The research into digital libraries is rich, and we hope that ILS vendors are taking note. From innovative user interfaces, to alternative search tools, to machine classification algorithms, to multi-lingual vocabulary mapping, many ideas and research programs are documented in the conference proceedings edited by Marchionini. For our users we must include more content. It is not realistic to expect more staff and budget, so we must innovate without increasing expenses.

Automated Harvesting and Interoperability of Metadata

Metadata harvesting and crawling of electronic archives and Web-based depositories provides a means to increase our content. A good example is the "E-pub" project at the University of Florida (Su 171). In this project, metadata was extracted from a collection of electronic agricultural reports. This data was converted to MARC data and loaded into the library catalog. The basic concept is similar to the work we have done with Ford research publication, except that rather than gathering the metadata when the reports are published, a Web crawler gathered the data after the publication.

The Open Archives Initiative Metadata Harvesting Project (University of Illinois at Urbana-Champaign, "Open Archives Initiative Metadata Harvesting Project") is another such project that provides an architecture from which to gather "information objects." It would be exciting, especially for special libraries, to have metadata harvesting tools become standard utilities so that librarians can quickly and inexpensively improve access to electronic archives that are of interest to their user base.

The Metadata Switch (OCLC, "Metadata Switch") project, which is sponsored by OCLC, explores how we can navigate through the various kinds of metadata, be it Dublin Core, ONIX, METS, MODS, XML, or MARC. Metadata can be harvested, re-used, and converted from one scheme to another in order to incorporate content. It is our hope that the ILS vendors are paying attention to such projects.

Improvements to the User Interface

A recent article states that libraries have 21st century users but 20th century catalogs (Theimer 11). The 20th century catalog does not note misspellings, but Google does. The 20th century catalog does not make full use of the complexity and richness of a controlled vocabulary such as a subject heading system. Semantic indexing and exploitation of semantic relationships in thesauri can facilitate the expansion of terms (Tudhope 84).

Data visualization and mapping is an intriguing possibility for the OPAC. Rather than the standard presentation of a list of sources, a visual presentation of resources is more like a topographical map. For a fascinating presentation of a visual catalog, see the online catalog for the library at Belmont Abbey College (http://belmont.antarcti.ca/). Data visualization has been used for a number of years to understand very large data sets, and to see literally patterns of data, patterns that cannot be readily understood from a list.

Open URL, Open Source

The Open URL standard being developed by NISO (National Information Standards Organization (http://www.niso.org/committees/committee_ax.html) is an exciting development that offers many possibilities for context-sensitive linking and extending the availability of related resources. ILS vendors are starting to incorporate compliance into products.

The open source philosophy, whereby developers provide the source code of the product instead of keeping it locked up and proprietary, is making its way into the ILS. Only a small clutch of such systems exist, and they are not as feature-rich as the traditional proprietary turnkey operation. However, this is a trend worth watching because, with availability of the source code, and a price that is right, open source systems could be a large source of innovation.

CONCLUSION

The integrated library system emerged from a rich process of innovation, and this innovation has been beneficial to libraries. In terms of presentation to user communities, the ILS has been eclipsed by the larger "space" of digital libraries and Web databases. The ILS need not be a poor relation when compared to other Web services. It is a rich database that uses a flexible system of metadata. It can be used for much more than a parochial tracking system of books and journals. There are interesting research and capability in the larger world of digital libraries. This innovation needs to be incorporated into next-generation systems, as well as the innovative custom applications that have been developed by individual libraries. The digital library has been another spectacular development for libraries, but it can be an unwieldy tool that requires significant management time. There is opportunity for the ILS to become a more central resource of the digital library given a richer set of utilities and increased flexibility.

WORKS CITED

Breeding, Marshall. "Capturing the Migration Customer." *Library Journal*, 127 (2002): 48-60.

Danskin, Alan. "Today MARC Harmonisation, Tomorrow the World Wide Web: UKMARC, MARC21, XML and ONIX." *Catalogue & Index* 143 (2002): 1-3.

Jacobs, Eva E., ed. *The Handbook of U.S. Labor Statistics*. 6th ed. Lanham, MD: Bernan Press, 2003.

Marchionini, Gary and William Hersh, eds. *Proceedings of the Second ACS/IEEE-CS Joint Conference on Digital Libraries*. New York: ACM: 2002.

Matthews, Joseph R. "The Value of Information: The Case of the Library Catalog." *Technical Services Quarterly* 19 (2001): 1-16.

Milsap, Larry. "A History of the Online Catalog in North America." *Technical Services Management 1965-1990*. New York: The Haworth Press, Inc.: 1996. 79-91.

Morris, Dilys E. and Gregory J. Wool. "Cataloging: Librarianship's Best Bargain." *Library Journal*, 124 (1999): 44-46.

OCLC. *Metadata Switch*. 2002. 4 April 2003 <http://www.oclc.org/research/projects/mswitch/index.shtm>.

Sloan, Bernard G. "Ten Years After: Lessons from a Decade of Automated Resource Sharing." *IOLS '89 Proceedings*. Medford, NJ: Learned Information Inc, 1989. 145-148.

Spicher, Karen M. "The Development of the MARC Format." *Cataloging & Classification Quarterly* 21(1996): 75-90.

Su, Siew-Phek T., Yu Long and Daniel E. Cromwell, "E2M: Automatic Generation of MARC-Formatted Metadata by Crawling e-Publications." *Information Technology and Libraries*, 21 (2002): 171-80.

Terrell, Tom. "Salaries Rebound, Women Break Out: Placements and Salaries 2001." *Library Journal* 127 (2002): 30-34,36.

Theimer, Sarah. "When a 21st Century User Meets a 20th Century OPAC: How Word Choice Impacts Search Success." *PNLA Quarterly*, 66 (2002): 11-12.

Tudhope, Douglas, Ceri Binding, Dorothee Blocks, and Daniel Cunliffe. "Compound Descriptors in Context: A Matching Function for Classifications and Thesauri." *Proceedings of the Second ACS/IEEE-CS Joint Conference on Digital Libraries.* New York: ACM: 2002. 84-93.

The University of Illinois at Urbana-Champaign. *Open Archives Initiative Metadata Harvesting Project.* 3 April 2003. 4 April 2003 <http://oai.grainger.uiuc.edu/index.htm>.

The University of Texas at Austin. General Libraries. *The Library Acquisitions Overview.* Dec. 2001. 4 April 2003 <http://www.lib.utexas.edu/admin/cird/acquisitionsoverview.html>.

Williams, Robert V. "The Use of Punched Cards in US Libraries and Documentation Centers, 1936-1972." *IEEE Annals of the History of Computing* 24 (2002): 16-33.

Shifting Priorities:
Print and Electronic Serials
at The University of Montana

Michelle S. Millet
Susan Mueller

SUMMARY. Following a library-wide brainstorming session and retreat, the Dean of the Maureen and Mike Mansfield Library tasked an ad-hoc committee to discuss implications for the library and its users if certain processes were implemented or eliminated in order to streamline the processing of serials. As the library's collection continues to shift from print to electronic, the processing of serials needs to shift with it. This paper focuses on the committee and its deliberations, as it discussed the state of electronic and print journals at The University of Montana. *[Article copies available for a fee from The Haworth Document Delivery Service: 1-800-HAWORTH. E-mail address: <docdelivery@haworthpress.com> Website: <http://www.HaworthPress.com> © 2006 by The Haworth Press, Inc. All rights reserved.]*

Michelle S. Millet is Assistant Professor, Information Literacy Coordinator, Elizabeth Hugh Coates Library, Trinity University, One Trinity Place, San Antonio, TX 78212-7200 (E-mail: Michelle.Millet@Trinity.edu). Susan Mueller is Director of Technical Services, Maureen and Mike Mansfield Library, The University of Montana, Missoula, MT 59812-9936 (E-mail: mueller@selway.umt.edu).

[Haworth co-indexing entry note]: "Shifting Priorities: Print and Electronic Serials at The University of Montana." Millet, Michelle S., and Susan Mueller. Co-published simultaneously in *The Acquisitions Librarian* (The Haworth Information Press, an imprint of The Haworth Press, Inc.) No. 35/36, 2006, pp. 135-147; and: *Integrating Print and Digital Resources in Library Collections* (ed: Audrey Fenner) The Haworth Information Press, an imprint of The Haworth Press, Inc., 2006, pp. 135-147. Single or multiple copies of this article are available for a fee from The Haworth Document Delivery Service [1-800-HAWORTH, 9:00 a.m. - 5:00 p.m. (EST). E-mail address: docdelivery@haworthpress.com].

Available online at http://www.haworthpress.com/web/AL
© 2006 by The Haworth Press, Inc. All rights reserved.
Digital Object Identifier: 10.1300/J101v18n35_10

KEYWORDS. Electronic journals, collection development, serials processing, e-journals

INTRODUCTION

Not so long ago, electronic periodicals were considered an experimental format. Libraries were willing to try them out, add them to the array of formats and materials available for their users, but not abandon the tried and true method of providing access to current issues and archives of a journal in print format. Libraries continued to subscribe to the print version, as well as acquire the electronic version of journals. The publishing community was just as unsure of electronic formats. Would electronic journals do away with their source of revenue? As a hedge against this possible scenario, many publishers responded by requiring that libraries continue to purchase the print version in order to get a favorable cost for the electronic version.

A new dilemma arose out of this desire to continue to provide access to journal articles in print, the historic model, and the industry's fear of losing a major source of revenue. Libraries were now put into the position of not only handling print versions of journals in the same way as before, but they also had the burden of managing a new format with very few guidelines on how to accomplish that. To this day, most libraries continue to struggle with the management of electronic serials. Many have added new staff to take on the additional workload or shifted existing staff to take care of new priorities. Other libraries have used third party vendors to manage their electronic subscriptions, while others have simply not addressed this whole new arena to the fullest extent.

At the Maureen and Mike Mansfield Library of The University of Montana, library management, faculty, and staff took an interesting approach to this problem. After a library-wide brainstorming session brought forth the management of serials, electronic and print, as an important concern to the library and its users, an ad-hoc committee was formed to deal with several issues. A committee of staff and faculty from various departments came together to brainstorm about the state of serials subscriptions at the Mansfield Library. From the committee's deliberations, implications and outcomes were put forth to the Dean for action and possible ways to solve the serials issue. While library management made the final decisions regarding serials processing and moved some items to the collection development team, the focus of this article is the process our library and the ad-hoc committee undertook to discuss and uncover the best ways to manage serials.

THE LIBRARY:
NEW DEAN, NEW GOALS, NEW ENVIRONMENT FUTURE

The Maureen and Mike Mansfield Library of The University of Montana has been undergoing a shift in priorities for the past three years, concentrating on user-focused services. In tandem with the addition of new online academic databases and electronic journals, came a new Dean of Library Services to lead the Mansfield Library into the next millennium. Wrestling with issues relating to acquisitions and collection development is a constant problem that begets additional concerns. Some of the issues facing the Mansfield Library include: providing access to electronic journals and the management of electronic resources, cancellation of print sources for electronic, and questioning whether to process the print collection in the same manner.

Academic libraries everywhere are struggling to remain relevant on campus and the Mansfield Library is not immune to this. With the advent of the Internet, the academic library now has competition, even in the previously sacred arena of academic research. Current students access their libraries electronically and are demanding more full-text access to academic resources. In 2002, OCLC commissioned a study and determined that "college and university students look to campus libraries and library Web sites for their information needs" ("How Academic" 1). By accepting this notion, and ensuring that students are also introduced to the concepts of information literacy, libraries will not just prove their worth and relevance, they will move into the future with their students and faculty.

One way to remain relevant is through a library's mission statement. The Mansfield Library administration implemented a library-wide retreat in order to discuss the library's strengths and weaknesses, goals and mission. The retreat came together in phases: a brainstorming session to bring forth the ideas most important to the entire library, followed by a committee and subcommittees to discuss the outcomes, and then the physical daylong retreat where the brainstorming and committee outcomes were put forth to the library (see Appendix).

The answers to the library-wide brainstorming brought the issue of electronic journals to the forefront. At the heart of the discussion was the problem of accessing the library's electronic subscriptions and maintaining these resources. Management realized that this particular issue must take a high priority, as the electronic resources portion of the budget was increasing at a rapid rate, while they were also getting the most use.

At the library wide-retreat, we were fortunate to have two guest speakers, Rick Anderson and Olivia Sullivan from the University of Nevada-Reno, who discussed with us many of the same issues they had with journal management. While not all examples of change that occurred at UN-Reno were applicable to the Mansfield Library, one of the overall themes from their presentation prompted the Mansfield Library to review and possibly change the way it physically processed serials. The expected outcome would allow the library to more thoroughly maintain access to electronic products, which are in higher demand, and remain relevant to our campus community. It became apparent that the library could not continue to maintain all of the same print journal processes, at current staffing levels, as well as tackle the task of management of electronic products. There were additional concerns relating to the discussion of online and print products. Do we, as a library, continue to keep "double" subscriptions in both print and electronic form? Should the library continue to subscribe to national newspapers in print when subscriptions to electronic resources provide the full text of those sources?

THE AD-HOC COMMITTEE

The result of the retreat was the formulation of an ad-hoc committee to review implications of specific processes, put forth by the Dean, relating to serials. Most relevant to this discussion are the following items the committee was asked to answer.

What are the implications to the library and library users if:

- Paid periodical print subscriptions are cancelled whenever the library secures a paid electronic subscription;
- With the exception of regional and Montana newspapers, current subscriptions to newspapers are received in electronic rather than print form;
- Print newspaper backfiles are maintained for no more than thirty days and users are directed to access newspaper backfiles electronically; and

- An additional agenda item, added as a chair's prerogative, was the shift of the management of electronic serials from a professional librarian to support staff in the serials department.

Because the discussion of serials included current processes and a shift in workflow, more specific processes in the committee's charge included implications of the following:

- Check-in and claiming is done for only a select number of paid print subscriptions; and
- Most periodical gift and exchange activities are discontinued.

The Dean designed the make-up of the committee so that all facets of the library would be represented, including both public and technical services. Of the ten committee members, there were staff members and faculty librarians, to ensure input from a variety of staffing levels, including two staff members from the serials department, a staff member of the systems department, a staff member responsible for binding, a staff member and the department head of Interlibrary Loan, the head of technical services, two public services librarians, and an administrative member of the Library Management Group (LMG). Both authors were members of the committee.

SHIFTING FROM PRINT TO ELECTRONIC SERIALS

Just as libraries worldwide are struggling with issues relating to print journals, electronic journals, and duplication, so is the Mansfield Library. While the goal of the ad-hoc committee was not just to deal with the issue of electronic journal management or solely with electronic journals, it became apparent that these topics were both serious issues for our library.

When considering the Mansfield Library's biggest constituents, faculty, staff, and students, the library faculty and staff realizes that most people prefer to access journals electronically. Results of a recent survey of college faculty and students showed that faculty was most likely to pursue information "in their offices" and "undergraduates in their residences" (Viles 766). OCLC's survey of students also found that most students used full-text journal articles and that full-text electronic journals accounted for 67% of what college students utilized from the library electronically ("How Academics" 6). Librarians at the University of Michigan also found similar results after conducting a two-year research study concerning journal usage among social science faculty on their campus. The majority of faculty members served were enthusiastic about electronic journals and what they have to offer (Palmer and Sandler 26).

THE CHANGING NATURE OF SERIALS PROCESSING

When considering the question of whether or not to continue to manage the serials collection in the same manner as in the past, a literature search was conducted. What was found is that changing the way libraries and librarians process serials is a fairly new concept and the discussion of the process of checking-in serials, an important piece of the process, is so ingrained in the whole workflow that there is little discussion of the process at all in the current literature. In a recent article by Mark Horan, a detailed report of the development of an automated check-in system is discussed, but there is no question about the need to do this activity. Other articles on serials management discuss the activity as a foregone conclusion with no debate as to its usefulness, only as to the best way to do it. Getting closer to the topic is the article by Montgomery and Sparks. Their report outlines some of the organizational changes necessitated by a transition to an electronic journal collection. With their article they state:

> In transitioning to an electronic format, there is a decrease in the staffing needs, and thereby in operational costs, associated with maintaining print journal collections. Shelving, stack maintenance, support for photocopying, manual statistics collection, journal check-in, claiming, and binding are all reduced. (Montgomery 10)

Though this acknowledges a transition from standard practice, it seems only to emphasize that there is less of these activities because of fewer retained print titles, rather than a decision to alter the activities.

The first instance of a total change of thinking in this area came in the one page article in *Library Journal* written by Rick Anderson (56). He reported on his institution's decision to give up checking-in serials as a routine activity and relegate it to only those items that are both high cost and high use. Discussions within the library serials community on this new direction for a routine process were aired within the SERIALST listserv between Aug. 13, 2002 and Aug. 18, 2002. The hue and cry was loud among many of the participants, who truly thought of the elimination of check-in as unthinkable. Concerns about auditing, claiming, and binding were also discussed in addition to the main focal point of no longer checking-in journals. Anderson went on to outline this in more detail in his article "Implementing the Unthinkable: The Demise of Periodicals Check-In at the University of Nevada." In this article Anderson detailed the decisions reached by the Vice President for Information Technology and Dean of Libraries, Steven Zink, and himself. Anderson also conducted a literature review and found essentially the same environment as noted above (63).

COMMITTEE DELIBERATIONS

The committee met over a period of two and half months to discuss each and every implication to all scenarios suggested by the Dean. Some of the committee's deliberations included detailed discussions, prompted by articles put forth by the chair of the committee. Each meeting took a different aspect of the questions posed by the Dean to address. This allowed the committee to focus on specific aspects of the serials dilemma. By having a diverse group of individuals on the committee it was truly a learning exercise. Looking at print and electronic serials from various points of view and library service points allowed each of us to become better informed as to how complex this situation had become.

The committee then took the meat of their discussions and summarized the implications to each question. The implications to the library concerning the handling of serials were noted first and then the implications to the users and how a scenario would benefit or hinder access to the materials. Once these were summarized and agreed upon by the committee, the three-page document was submitted to the Dean.

MANAGEMENT OF ELECTRONIC SERIALS: SHIFTING RESPONSIBILITIES

The current process of management of electronic serials was not a direct point of discussion for the committee charged by the Dean, but one put forth at the discretion of the chair. Before the committee's deliberations, electronic subscriptions were acquired through a serials technician, but the Electronic Resources Librarian, a member of the ad-hoc committee, set up the maintenance and public access. The Mansfield Library had contracted with SerialsSolutions in 2002 and the librarian added any new electronic journals, through aggregators or publishers, to the current list. She also connected each electronic journal package to the library's online abstract and index databases.

As the committee discussed the processes the serials department currently undertook, it became apparent that some of the processes performed by support staff for print serials were being done by a professional librarian for electronic serials. If the committee was discussing the best practices to get all of the library's serials processed, it seemed apparent to the committee that the serials department should begin to process electronic as well as print serials. For the Electronic Resources Librarian, this made sense because the serials department had contact with vendors and subscription agents and could easily access the information necessary when connecting electronic subscriptions.

CONCLUSIONS

Pertinent to the previously mentioned tasks charged by the Dean, the ad-hoc committee detailed the following implications for the library and library users if the actions studied were implemented. For the purposes of this paper, only the issues relating to the management of print and electronic periodicals will be discussed.

1. *Paid periodical print subscriptions are canceled whenever the Library secures a paid electronic subscription for the same title.* The committee found that the library would benefit from less staff time being devoted to processing duplicate print titles, but that may balance out with the processing of electronic journals. The group also decided that canceling print might cause the library to lose backfile access. Users would benefit from electronic access because it provides for multiple simultaneous user access, and electronic access may provide faster access than waiting for the print journals to be processed. It was also noted by the committee that faculty members across campus often demand electronic journals, so that they can access them from their offices. It was stressed by the committee, however, that cancellation of print in favor of electronic subscriptions will not include aggregator databases, such as Academic Index or Lexis-Nexis, because they do not provide consistent content or stable archives, as noted by other libraries (Sprague and Chambers 29).

2. *With the exception of regional and Montana newspapers, current subscriptions to newspapers are received in electronic, rather than print, format.* The Mansfield Library currently subscribes to eighty-six newspapers in print. The committee noted a possible cost savings if newspapers were cancelled, including the cost of the subscriptions and supplies for maintenance and check-in. However, the cost of acquiring online subscriptions might cancel that benefit. Both serials and circulation staff would benefit because time and energy is currently spent on processing, shelving, and removing newspapers. The library would also be able to free up shelving space, a current need. For users, accessing newspapers electronically would allow them faster access and the bulk of our users already access most newspapers that way. Of course, some newspapers may not be available in electronic format and those that are, do not always provide backfile access. The ad-hoc committee also recommended that the collection development team evaluate some of the foreign language newspapers that the library currently receives and assess the need, campus-wide.

3. *Newspaper print backfiles are maintained for not more than thirty days and users are directed to access newspaper backfiles electronically.* The committee noted that, again, acquiring newspapers electronically would mean that less staff time would be devoted to maintaining the backfiles. However, backfiles can be very costly in electronic format or may not be available. Users would benefit because the committee thought the OPAC display would be easier to understand if all newspapers were kept for thirty days, without exceptions. Currently, papers are usually kept for six months, but this can vary depending on the publication. The committee also recommended that the library continue subscriptions to the microform newspapers to which it subscribes and that users be directed to access backfiles of newspapers in whatever non-print format the library selects.

4. *The management of electronic serials moves from the Electronic Resources Librarian to the serials department.* This added agenda item came to the forefront because it seemed that the overall discussion of print periodicals and their management coincided with the management of electronic serials. By combining the management of both types of serials into one department, both the library and its users benefit. Because the serials department is used to handling issues relating to the processing of serials, including purchasing, invoicing, contacting vendors with problems, and assisting library faculty and staff, it seemed like a natural migration to move the processing of electronic serials to their department.

It will take work on the part of the Electronic Resources Librarian and the serials technicians to make the migration of work a smooth transition, but it will be beneficial to the library in the end. Overall workflow in serials may need to be examined and administrative details need to be taken care of. The committee decided that the effects on the users, if any, would be minimal. Users would not be affected by who manages the electronic serials; however, if the serials unit could accomplish more than a single librarian, users would benefit from increased access.

Once the committee provided the Dean with its report of possible implications to the scenarios involving serials, any final decisions were up to him. The Dean took the document to the Library Management Group (LMG), the senior management group within the library. This group includes the Directors of Public and Technical Services as well as the Director of the College of Technology Library, the online catalog system administrator, the technology administrator, the Associate Director of Administrative, Fiscal and Personnel Services, the Access Services Coordinator, the Information Services Coordinator, and the Dean. The chair of the task force provided a commentary on the document and answered any questions the LMG had about the process and the outcomes. Once this was done, the Dean identified areas of the report that would go on to the collection development team for further resolution. He also made decisions about other aspects of the report.

The areas that were forwarded to the collection development team for resolution included:

- Review of the library gifts policy, with special emphasis on reviewing the donation of serials;
- Review of the current policy of displaying some journal issues in a separate area apart from previous volumes;
- Review the practice of routing library journals;
- Review the practice of manually claiming and invoicing serials and possibly replace it with electronic procedures;
- Review duplication of paper and electronic versions of journals;
- Review subscriptions to both a print and electronic version of national newspapers; and
- Review the practice of managing electronic serials by the electronic resources librarian rather than by the serials department.

The most significant aspect of the deliberations that was not forwarded to the collection development team pertained to the check-in of paper serials. With the realization that someone would still need to look up each issue for a call number, it was determined by the Dean that not checking-in the journals would not save that much time or effort. Also, it was not in the library's best interest to eliminate check-in at this time because our journals are categorized within the library in a different way than at the University of Nevada-Reno, the model the ad-hoc committee examined.

Of those areas that were forwarded to the collection development team, some were easily resolved. For example, internal routing of library journals was ceased, as most of them were available either online in full text or the table of contents was available electronically. The collection development team began reviewing the library's collection development policy while the serials ad-hoc committee deliberated; therefore, the portion of the policy pertaining to gifts was reviewed as part of the process. It was also determined that journals on display throughout the library required more handling than was necessary and will be integrated into the collection at the end of the semester. During the deliberations of the ad-hoc committee, transition from manual claiming and invoicing to electronic claiming and invoicing began and was in place by the time LMG received the report.

Some last items from the original charge of the ad-hoc committee needed resolutions. They included the following:

- The collection development team asked for more detailed information on the number and titles of the journals that are duplicated in print and electronically. With this information the collection development team will determine the feasibility of canceling additional paper subscriptions. The same is true for the newspapers. Once it is detailed as to the cost of substituting electronic access for print access, decisions regarding duplication will be made. This process will be on the agenda for the collection development team beginning May 2003.
- Finally, the responsibility for electronic serials management will be transferred as soon as it receives the approval of the Dean.

Overall, this exercise proved to be worthwhile. It provided a venue for those with concerns about the direction the library was taking with the management of print and electronic serials. It provided a means to get to the gist of the matter so that it could be discussed in a meaningful way. The committee and the Mansfield Library have gone beyond looking at serials check-in and other aspects of serials management as routine and invisible. We now have explored the hows and whys of these activities.

REFERENCE

Anderson, Rick. "Re: Quit Checking in Journal Issues?" Online posting. 13 Aug. 2002. SERIALST. 18 Feb. 2003.

_____. "A Sacred Cow Bites the Dust." *Library Journal* (1 May 2002): 56.

Anderson, Rick and Steven D. Zink. "Implementing the Unthinkable: The Demise of Periodical Check-In at the University Of Nevada." *Library Collections, Acquisitions, and Technical Services* 27.1 (2003): 61-71.

Horan, Mark. "Building a Serials Check-In Datafile Using Microsoft Access and Paper Check In Principles." *Serials Review* 26.1 (2000): 22-42.

"How Academic Librarians Can Influence Students' Web-Based Information Choices." *OCLC White Paper on the Information Habits of College Students*. OCLC Online Computer Library Center, Inc., 2002. 10 Feb. 2003 <http://www2.oclc.org/oclc/pdf/printondemand/informationhabits.pdf>.

Montgomery, Carol H. and JoAnne Sparks. "The Transition to an Electronic Journal Collection: Managing the Organizational Changes." *Serials Review* 26.3 (2000): 4-18.

Palmer, Janet P. and Mark Sandler. "What Do Faculty Want?" *Library Journal NetConnect* (Winter 2003): 26-28.

Sprague, Nancy and Mary Beth Chambers. "Full-Text Databases and the Journal Cancellation Process: A Case Study." *Serials Review* 26.3 (2000): 19-31.

Viles, Ann. "Fast Facts: Information Access on Campus." *College & Research Libraries News* 63.10 (November 2002): 766.

APPENDIX. Brainstorming Questions Posed to All Faculty and Staff of the Mansfield Library

1. How would you reshape library services to meet the emerging and actual needs of our constituents?
2. How would you reshape library operations to meet the emerging and actual needs of our constituents?
3. What opportunities and skills do you need to develop your potential as an employee?
4. How do we foster a better environment to promote employee and patron diversity?
5. What can we do for our affiliated and external constituencies? What can they do for us?
6. How do we build assessment into everything we do?
7. How do we facilitate more effective communication both internally and externally?
8. Given the preceding discussion how should our Mission Statement be added to/deleted/changed?

The Library and the Faculty Senate: Legitimizing the Serials Evaluation Process Using the Department of Biology Subscriptions

Sandhya D. Srivastava
Pamela Harpel-Burke

SUMMARY. This article documents the process used by the Hofstra University's Library and Faculty Senate to evaluate current serials title lists for different academic departments. The library has found that initiating this effort through the auspices of the Faculty Senate Library Subcommittee (FSLS) allows it to create an environment of legitimate concern and respect. The faculty also feels that their needs and concerns

Sandhya D. Srivastava is Serials Librarian (E-mail: librsds@hofstra.edu); and Pamela Harpel-Burke is Catalog Librarian (E-mail: libctphb@hofstra.edu), both at Axinn Library, Hofstra University, Hempstead, NY 11549.

The authors would like to thank Deborah Dolan, MLS; Howard Graves, Assistant Dean for Technical Services; Russell Burke, PhD, Department of Biology, Hofstra University; Ari Cohen, MLS, Long Island University Brooklyn Campus; Paolina Taglienti, MLS, New York Academy of Medicine; and Audrey Fenner (editor), for all of their help in editing the final copy of this article. The authors would also like to thank Daniel R. Rubey, PhD, Dean of Libraries, Hofstra University.

[Haworth co-indexing entry note]: "The Library and the Faculty Senate: Legitimizing the Serials Evaluation Process Using the Department of Biology Subscriptions." Srivastava, Sandhya D., and Pamela Harpel-Burke. Co-published simultaneously in *The Acquisitions Librarian* (The Haworth Information Press, an imprint of The Haworth Press, Inc.) No. 35/36, 2006, pp. 149-159; and: *Integrating Print and Digital Resources in Library Collections* (ed: Audrey Fenner) The Haworth Information Press, an imprint of The Haworth Press, Inc., 2006, pp. 149-159. Single or multiple copies of this article are available for a fee from The Haworth Document Delivery Service [1-800-HAWORTH, 9:00 a.m. - 5:00 p.m. (EST). E-mail address: docdelivery@haworthpress.com].

Available online at http://www.haworthpress.com/web/AL
© 2006 by The Haworth Press, Inc. All rights reserved.
Digital Object Identifier: 10.1300/J101v18n35_11

149

about the library collection are heard and validated by the presence of the Dean of Libraries and the Assistant Dean of Technical Services. The process is designed to allow effective serials evaluation by all parties involved. The faculty has input by asking for cancellations and additions based on lists created using an Access 2000 database. These lists contain title information, price, and use statistics. The article also presents the events that occurred November 5, 2002, when the library and the Department of Biology had their initial evaluation meeting with the Chair of the FSLS in attendance. *[Article copies available for a fee from The Haworth Document Delivery Service: 1-800-HAWORTH. E-mail address: <docdelivery@haworthpress.com> Website: <http://www.HaworthPress.com>* © 2006 by The Haworth Press, Inc. All rights reserved.]

KEYWORDS. Academic libraries, biology journals, collection management databases, e-journals, electronic resources, faculty senate, library liaison, serials evaluation

INTRODUCTION

This article documents the process for collection development and management of serials at Hofstra University. Since library budgets are now more static, this process is an essential consideration for any academic library. Libraries now have to find better ways of using their serials budgets to further their buying power to meet curriculum needs. Using funds budgeted for monographs to cover serials subscriptions is becoming a more frequent occurrence in libraries (Miller 1).

In 1999, the Faculty Senate Library Subcommittee (referred to as FSLS throughout) of Hofstra University implemented a serials evaluation project which will continue until all academic departments undergo the process. The major goal of this procedure is to assure that the serials collection is supporting the department needs for their curriculum based needs of the university. Since the needs of any department would change over time, it was necessary to come up with a process that would allow initial collection review as well as follow-up reviews (Burke 39).

A relevant point to this discussion is the fact that the library at Hofstra University changed its collection development process recently as a result of needs identified by the FSLS and the Dean of Libraries (referred to as the Dean from this point). In the year 2000, a library liaison system was implemented. The duties of the subject specialist (librarian in our liaison system) now include collection development and management of the book, serials, and electronic resources collections.

The authors of this article culled the literature to see if other libraries supported similar practices and to review what procedures had been documented in the library literature on the serials collection development and management procedures. In an academic setting, the process of evaluating serials was generally left solely to the library faculty with little input from the teaching faculty unless specifically requested by the department. As an example of the serials evaluation process now underway at Hofstra University, this article will document the process for the Department of Biology.

REVIEW OF THE LITERATURE

A review of the professional literature on collection development as it pertains to serials yielded a variety of approaches different from that of Hofstra University. Not surprisingly, many of the articles focused on evaluating a serials collection via the method of using ISI's *Journal Citation Reports* to determine the most highly cited journals in a given subject area. Websites of academic libraries were also reviewed for collection development policies. However, many libraries did not specifically address serials evaluation procedures. Lack of information on serials management (and collection development procedures in general) may be due to several factors, such as, the internal nature of library documentation, procedures still being formulated, administration reaction to crisis-oriented events, or simply that it has been ignored.

A few institutions, such as the Oregon Health & Science University Library, however, presented a more comprehensive approach to journal selection. Regardless of the reasons, the literature and Web sites did not reveal an approach that combined all of the components of Hofstra University serials evaluation procedures. Administrative support and the backing of a university's governing body, such as the faculty senate, accounts for the success of our process.

Collection development literature did recognize the importance of forging and maintaining strong alliances with the faculty (Swigger and Wilkes 3-4; Kotter 2; Metz and Cosgriff 2). In most cases, the liaison model was rarely applied to the serials collection. Serials decisions were considered the purview of technical services departments rather than library liaisons.

In addition to journal citations as a method for justifying or collecting specific titles, many libraries focused on usage studies or shelving statistics. Specific user needs were not ignored. Metz and Cosgriff addressed specific needs by conducting a survey of the faculty. These needs were also compared to actual usage data. Although it has been argued that the teaching faculty do not always have a clear picture of their needs (Birdsall 1), librarians would be remiss to ignore teaching faculty as a valuable resource. In addition to faculty needs, Metz and Cosgriff looked at shelving data and ISI's *Journal Citation Reports* to build a "comprehensive decision-support database bringing together all known elements about given resources" (Metz and Cosgriff 1).

Other approaches have been used to examine the need for electronic versus print journals. Literature suggests that many of the science faculty and students in academic libraries prefer electronic format over print (Hurd, Blecic, and Vishwanatham 5; Tobia 8). Brennan, Hurd, Blecic, and Weller also noted that scientists liked the timeliness and added value for multimedia capabilities of e-journals. Currency, rapid retrieval and power of searching also drive these preferences.

This is not to say that the faculty has been ignored in collection development processes. Bosch and Jones outlined how the University of Arizona used their Faculty Senate to determine cancellation of titles. They also briefly described the process of consulting their Faculty Senate as well as the production of a database to achieve necessary cancellations (Bosch and Jones 1). Although this does not seem to be an ongoing practice for collection development of their library's serials, it is similar to Hofstra University's serials evaluation process.

COLLECTION DEVELOPMENT
PROCESS AND PROCEDURES

The collection development process initially starts with a review of the journal list for the department in cooperation with the FSLS. This procedure begins when the subject specialist or library subcommittee chair requests a current department journal list from the Serials Librarian. The requestor forwards the list to the department chair and the department liaison. After the department performs its own review of the current journal list, they contact the subject specialist or the library subcommittee chair with their recommendations for cancellations and additions. At this point, they may also choose to request pricing for new titles that they want to add to the collection (Rubey 1).

The Serials Librarian then provides price quotes for all formats for the titles (print, print/online, online subscriptions). The list of requested additions is then forwarded to the Dean, subject specialist, or library subcommittee chair who originally processed the department request. It will then be forwarded to the department liaison and the department chair. The Dean contacts the Chair of the library subcommittee to arrange a meeting with the department as a whole (Rubey 1).

The purpose of the meeting is to discuss how to balance the cancellations with the additions that are necessary to make a better collection for the program curriculum. It is also an opportunity for the department to prioritize their "wish list" of new titles for a time when additional funds can be obtained. The library will discontinue all titles for which cancellation is requested and add new titles as funding allows. The decision whether to delete the cancelled title and holdings from the collection will be discussed as well (Rubey, p. 1). The faculty's incentive for agreeing to cut journals has to include a compromise to use some saved funds for these new journals. Both sides must trust each other to act in good faith. This trust is extremely delicate and represents a crucial part of the serials evaluation process.

The Chair of the library subcommittee attends the meeting which is an important aspect of our process. The department chair will designate attending members of the department group. It is usually recommended that the chair and the department liaison attend the meeting as well as any other interested department faculty. The library constituency consists of the Dean, Assistant Dean of Technical Services, the Serials Librarian and the subject specialist.

CREATING CURRENT JOURNAL LISTS

In 1999, the Department of Biology cancellation candidates were derived from two lists: an "over $500" list and an "over $200" list. The first list consisted of titles with costs over $500 with less than ten uses over the past year. The second list included titles between $200-$499 with usage of less than five times over the past year (Burke 39).

Due to the fact that cancelled and/or ceased titles were appearing on the current title lists sent to departments, an Access 2000 database was created. This Journals List database allowed the creation of department program lists. Because of its two fields of unique program codes, the Serials Librarian was able to create a query to find all titles that fall under a department program even those that are considered interdisciplinary. The query can be detailed to include title format, price, and user statistics. The database contains current titles only.

The use of Access 2000 to create a serials collection development tool made the task of creating the spreadsheet lists easier. In fact, it was very important to use this tool because Hofstra University's ILS (integrated library system) at this point does not have this capability. The ability to create program-coded lists allows our library the flexibility to work with the department in providing the information that they want to make their cancellation decisions.

BIOLOGY COLLECTION DEVELOPMENT MEETING

On November 5, 2002, the library constituency met with the Department of Biology to discuss their suggestions for cancellations and additions to their journal list. The Chair of the Senate Library Subcommittee also attended. The library group consisted of the Dean, the Assistant Dean of Technical Services and the Serials Librarian. The Department of Biology was represented by the department liaison, the department chair and two other teaching faculty who expressed interest in being part of the meeting.

The discussion began after the department liaison handed out two lists to all in attendance. One was a list of agreed cancellations made by all concurring biology teaching faculty and the second was a list of essential additions that the teaching faculty felt were necessary to their curriculum. The discussion began with the department liaison indicating that the Department of Biology wanted to change the format of their journals from paper to electronic. The faculty was more interested in accessing the article information for their classes. The library representatives were told that the electronic format was in fact easier to access and provided higher quality images than previously. Higher quality images combined with ready access to color printers meant that print journals were no longer needed. The Dean was open to the department's suggestions and was eager to support the transition to the electronic format.

Discussion shifted to the list of cancellations and how the library should deal with the de-accession of these titles. The department liaison indicated the faculty's willingness to remove back-runs of the paper as long as the previous years were available electronically. The discussion then moved to the list of potential additions. This was where the discussion became heated. One biology professor was adamant about how necessary it was for the Department of Biology to have the title *Cell* on its journal list. The faculty member indicated that this was the most prominent title needed to teach biology and it was absolutely necessary to have it in the library. The meeting ended with the agreement that the Serials Librarian would get pricing for electronic formats for the titles on the additions list and to see if the money from the cancelled titles would be able to offset the cost of titles to be added. Of the titles on the additions list, the library wanted to focus first on those that were mentioned as being essential to the biology collection. These were *BioMedNet Reviews*, *Cell*, *Cancer Cell*, *Developmental Cell*, *Current Biology*, *Molecular Cell*, *Nature*, *Nature Genetics*, *Nature Cell Biology*, *Nature Reviews Cancer*, and *Nature Reviews Molecular Cell Biology*.

One of the major problems that arose during this project was that there were interdisciplinary journals appearing on the biology title list. The number of pure biology titles that were initially cancelled was only fourteen from a list of 143 titles, which they indicated they did not want anymore (see Table 1).

The biology project essentially gave birth to an interdisciplinary title project. This project required the library to contact at least six other departments within three separate schools at Hofstra University concerning seventy titles which the Department of Biology deemed cancelable. The interdisciplinary project took over a month to receive all the decisions on the titles which was done through e-mails and internal department meetings. Finally, by mid-January 2003, all the e-mailed responses from all the departments were finalized for that project. Of the original titles on the list, the library was able to cancel only eight more of the 143 titles.

The original money saved from the fourteen pure biology titles was not enough to cover the amount needed to get all the titles on the biology additions list. However, it could cover subscriptions for *Nature*, *Cell*, and *BioMedNet Reviews* in electronic format. The Dean went back to the Biology Liaison to see if more titles could be cancelled or if the Department of Biology would be satisfied with the prospect of having access to the primary three packages they wanted as soon as possible. As it happened, the Department of Biology appreciated the efforts of the library to get this done so quickly.

With every step forward sometimes there is a step back. As the project continued, it was discovered that some of the titles which the Department of Biology wanted to keep had already been cancelled in the year 2000. Needless to say, this did introduce some tension into the project and greatly increased faculty unwillingness to participate in the

TABLE 1. Total dollars cancelled from Biology and Interdisciplinary lists, which covered the cost of the electronic journal and databases that were added to the Biology Department's journal list.

Biology Related Titles Cancelled	Price
BIOSIS Serial Sources	$ 160.00
Human Biology	$ 184.00
Human Development	$ 418.00
Human Genetics	$ 3,790.00
Journal of Motor Behavior	$ 163.00
Journal of Phycology	$ 479.00
Journal of the World Aquaculture Soc.	$ 105.00
Social Biology	$ 105.00
Aquaculture	$ 3,097.00
Aquaculture Europe	$ 57.00
Annual Review of Entomology	$ 163.00
Cortex	$ 190.00
International Wildlife	$ 26.00
Wilson Bulletin	$ 40.00
SUBTOTAL	$ 8,977.00
Interdisciplinary Titles Cancelled	
American Forests	$ 25.00
Bulletin of Environmental Contamination and Toxicology	$ 499.00
Environmental Science & Technology	$ 725.00
Journal of Environmental Economics and Management	$ 805.00
Journal of Environmental Quality	$ 204.00
Annals of Behavioral Medicine	$ 210.00
Journal of Affective Disorders	$ 2,267.00
Metabolism: Clinical & Experimental	$ 452.00
Radiology	$ 450.00
	$ 5,637.00
TOTAL	$14,614.00

process. This situation was addressed by the reinstatement of subscriptions for the current year but not purchase of the missing back-runs, which would require more funds. The interdisciplinary project resulted in extra funds becoming available which were then used to replace some of the missing years.

CONCLUSION

Although the idea of meeting face to face with department faculty may seem daunting, when it is done in the presence of the Chair of the FSLS and the Dean of Libraries, it brings legitimacy to the proceedings. Both the department and the library can arrive at good solutions that accommodate the needs of the department within the resources available to the library and the university. The process of serials evaluation can be a successful achievement that brings relevant issues to the forefront. The presence of the FSLS chair allows the aims and proceedings of the meeting to push forward instead of being bogged down with inconsequential issues. The presence of the Dean of Libraries allows the department to feel that their issues and grievances are being heard by someone who has the power to change the situation (or at least hear their point of view). Also, the Dean's presence signifies financial backing to any discussions based on budget and increases the legitimacy of the library's position in the discussion. The presence of the Assistant Dean of Technical Services ensures that the process and issues brought to the floor are dealt with, especially in issues related to pricing, lists, cancellations, and de-accession. He is also involved in electronic database purchases, and his knowledge of consortia arrangements adds additional influence to the decision-making process.

The Hofstra University serials evaluation process has increased the stature of the library within the university. The Dean of Library and Information Services has developed an evaluation procedure, which allows both the library and the teaching faculty to have crucial input and discussions about the serials collection, which affects the teaching of the curriculum. It takes both sides working together to make this a viable alternative. The serials evaluation process familiarizes teaching faculty with the budgetary realities of the library and why they cannot have everything they want. It allows all parties to make the best use of the available funds.

At the present time, the journal listings for Business Computer Information Systems, Physical Education & Sports Sciences, and Comparative Literature and Languages, Political Science, History, Sociology/Anthropology, Economics/Geography, and Geology Departments have been deemed complete by the current FSLS chair. The FSLS chair also wrote in the annual report to the Faculty Senate that the Departments of Chemistry and Biology were making progress on reviewing their journal listings (Mazzoleni 39). At the time of this article, the Department of Biology was very pleased to receive their new additions, but also made reference to the fact that they are still working on achieving more in the area of electronic databases and switching current paper subscriptions to electronic versions.

The FSLS renewed its commitment to the serials evaluation process in the Hofstra University Senate Annual Report when the Chair stated "while advancement has been made in the review process, the Subcommittee will be engaged in soliciting further involvement of the Hofstra faculty in the future" (Mazzoleni 39). The Chair affirmed that the summer and fall semesters would be used to contact Directors of the numerous interdisciplinary programs on campus about the journals review process (Mazzoleni 39). The statement underscored Hofstra University's focus on reviewing the serials collections of all of its programs and its continued commitment to supporting the curriculum.

LIST OF SELECTED RESOURCES

Ashcroft, Linda. "Issues in Developing, Managing and Marketing Electronic Journals Collections." *Collection Building* 21.4 (2002): 147-154.

Brennan, Martin J., Julie M. Hurd, Deborah D. Blecic, and Ann C. Weller. "A Snapshot of Early Adopters of E-Journals: Challenges to the Library." *College & Research Libraries* 63.6 (2002): 515-526.

Carroll, Diane. *Journal Selection Criteria*. Oregon Health & Science University. Collection Development Department. 27 Mar. 2003 <http://www.ohsu.edu/library/depts/colldevcomm/>.

Chu, Felix. "Librarian-Faculty Relations in Collection Development." *Journal of Academic Librarianship* 23.1 (1997): 15-20.

Dilevko, Juris and Esther Atkinson. (2002). "Evaluating Academic Journals Without Impact Factors for Collection Management Decisions." *College & Research Libraries* 63.6 (2002): 562-577.

Edwards, Sherri. "Citation Analysis as a Collection Development Tool: A Bibliometric Study of Polymer Science Theses and Dissertations." *Serials Review* 25.1 (1999): 11-20.

Lightman, Harriet with Sabina Malinov. "A Simple Method for Evaluating a Journal Collection: A Case Study of Northwestern University Library's Economics Collection." *Journal of Academic Librarianship* 26:3 (2000): 183-190.

Reichardt, Karen. "Using Microsoft Access for Journal Collection Development." *The Serials Librarian* 37.4 (2000): 69-78.

Rossignol, Lucien R. "Navigating the Waves of Change in Serials Management: Employing MS Access Database Management Software." *The Serials Librarian* 40.3/4 (2001): 267-270.

Zipp, Louise S. "Core Serial Titles in an Interdisciplinary Field: The Case of Environmental Geology." *Library Resources and Technical Services* 43.1 (1999): 28-36.

REFERENCES

Birdsall, W.F. "I Read, Therefore I Am: Faculty and the Psychology of Journal Cancellations." *Journal of Academic Librarianship* 24.3 (1999): 240-241.

Bosch, Steven and Doug Jones. "Attacking High-Inflation Serials–The University of Arizona Way." *Library Journal* 119.11 (6/15/94): 42-49.

Burke, Russell L. "Reports of the Committees of the Senate. Subcommittee on the Library." *Thirty-Sixth Annual Report of the Hofstra University Senate, 2000-2001.*

Hurd, Julie M., Deborah D. Blecic, and Rama Vishwanatham. "Information Use by Molecular Biologists: Implications for Library Collections and Services." *College & Research Libraries* 60.1 (1999): 31-43.

Kotter, Wade R. "Bridging the Great Divide: Improving Relations Between Librarians and Classroom Faculty." *Journal of Academic Librarianship* 25.2 (1999): 294-303.

Mazzoleni, Roberto. "Reports of the Committees of the Senate. Subcommittee on the Library." *Thirty-Seventh Annual Report of the Hofstra University Senate, 2001-2002.*

Metz, Paul and John Cosgriff. "Building a Comprehensive Serials Decision Database at Virginia Tech." *College & Research Libraries* 61.4 (2000): 324-334.

Miller, Ruth H. "Electronic Resources and Academic Libraries, 1980-2000." *Library Trends* 48.4 (2000): 645-670.

Rubey, Daniel. "Collection Development Procedures for Journals and Electronic Databases." Working paper, 8 Nov. 2002. Hofstra University Library.

Swigger, Keith and Adeline Wilkes. "The Use of Citation Data to Evaluate Serials Subscriptions in an Academic Library." *Serials Review* 91.2 (1991): 41-47.

Tobia, Rajia C. "Electronic Journals: Experiences of an Academic Health Sciences Library." *Serials Review* 27.1 (2001): 3-18.

21st Century Shell Game:
Cutting Serials in the Electronic Age

Richard P. Jasper

SUMMARY. The advent of online journals, bundled packages, and consortial "big deals" means that librarians have to work harder than ever when budget shortfalls require cutting serials. This article recounts the experience of the Houston Academy of Medicine-Texas Medical Center Library in its journal cancellation project of 2002. *[Article copies available for a fee from The Haworth Document Delivery Service: 1-800-HAWORTH. E-mail address: <docdelivery@haworthpress.com> Website: <http://www.HaworthPress.com> © 2006 by The Haworth Press, Inc. All rights reserved.]*

KEYWORDS. Aggregators, big deal, budget, bundled packages, cancellation, consortia, electronic journals, e-journals, serials

INTRODUCTION

Cutting journal subscriptions has always been a tricky business for libraries. For the most part we would just as soon cut off our fingers and

Richard P. Jasper is Director, Resource Services, Wayne State University Library System, Detroit, MI 48202 (E-mail: ap8401@wayne.edu).

[Haworth co-indexing entry note]: "21st Century Shell Game: Cutting Serials in the Electronic Age." Jasper, Richard P. Co-published simultaneously in *The Acquisitions Librarian* (The Haworth Information Press, an imprint of The Haworth Press, Inc.) No. 35/36, 2006, pp. 161-166; and: *Integrating Print and Digital Resources in Library Collections* (ed: Audrey Fenner) The Haworth Information Press, an imprint of The Haworth Press, Inc., 2006, pp. 161-166. Single or multiple copies of this article are available for a fee from The Haworth Document Delivery Service [1-800-HAWORTH, 9:00 a.m. - 5:00 p.m. (EST). E-mail address: docdelivery@haworthpress.com].

Available online at http://www.haworthpress.com/web/AL
© 2006 by The Haworth Press, Inc. All rights reserved.
Digital Object Identifier: 10.1300/J101v18n35_12

our toes as to have "gaps" in our collections. Determining what to cut, what to keep, how to balance the competing needs of faculty and students across disparate subject disciplines is an ongoing headache, especially in a publishing environment in which price increases have routinely and significantly outstripped the ability of libraries to keep pace.

The serials cancellation process has become even murkier thanks to the advent of electronic resources and more specifically bundled "big deal" packages and consortial purchasing agreements. Where previously librarians were faced with making decisions one title at a time, we are now confronted with a tangled thicket of print-to-electronic, title-to-package, package-to-consortium dynamics that seems to have no clear-cut answers. Add in loader fees, content fees, transaction fees, transaction allowances, cancellation restrictions, embargoed titles, multiple platforms, and we find ourselves confronting a whirling mass of unanswerable questions and unintended consequences.

It was against this backdrop in 2002 that the Houston Academy of Medicine-Texas Medical Center (HAM-TMC) Library had to plan a sizeable cut in its materials budget for 2003. As the HAM-TMC Library's Assistant Director for Collections during 1999-2002, I was for planning (in consultation with and subject to the approval of the Library's executive director) the serials cancellations for fiscal year 2002-2003. The HAM-TMC experience is recapitulated here for the many libraries throughout the United States that are currently having to undertake a similar process thanks to the dismal condition of state budgets and higher than average serials inflation predicted for 2004.

BACKGROUND

The HAM-TMC Library is the principal library for the Texas Medical Center, Inc., the world's largest medical complex. An independent, stand-alone library with its own governing Board of Directors, it is nonetheless the library of record for both the Baylor College of Medicine and the University of Texas-Houston Health Science Center.

The HAM-TMC Library is just one of several libraries serving the Texas Medical Center and the Houston-Galveston area. It is a member of the Texas Health Science Libraries Consortium (THSLC), which also includes the libraries of the UT MD Anderson Cancer Center, the UT Houston School of Public Health, the UT Psychiatry Branch, the UT Dental Branch, and (in Galveston) the UT Medical Branch. Thanks to its affiliation with the UT Houston Health Science Center, the

HAM-TMC Library is a fully participating member of the UT System Digital Library (UTSDL), which engages in collective purchasing of online resources for the 20-plus components of the UT System.

Over a three-year period beginning in the summer of 1999, the HAM-TMC Library quadrupled the number of online titles it made available to its users, from just fewer than 1,000 titles in June 1999 to a little more than 4,000 titles in early 2002. Although many of these titles were acquired through placing print plus electronic subscriptions through the Library's principal vendor, Swets Blackwell, more than half were the result of consortial purchases. The overwhelming majority of consortial purchases were made through UTSDL, although there were some significant exceptions involving THSLC or the South Central Association of Medical Libraries (SCAMEL).

In early 2002 it became apparent that the HAM-TMC Library was facing a significant revenue shortfall for FY 02/03. After much deliberation it was decided that a balanced budget could be achieved through a combination of salary savings from vacant positions and a significant cut (roughly $250,000) in expenditures for library materials.

EXAMINING OPTIONS

As with any health sciences library, the HAM-TMC Library's materials budget is overwhelmingly skewed towards serials, whether print or electronic or some combination thereof. During the period 1999-2002 only about 6-7% of the total materials budget, or less than $150,000 per year, was allocated for firm orders and approval plan materials. (During an earlier budget crunch in the mid 1990s the Library had already significantly cut back on its standing orders for monographic series titles.) Even if the entire budget for firm orders and approval plans had been eliminated the Library's target of a $250,000 reduction in materials expenditures would not have been met. Instead the Library opted for a sizeable cut in the book budget ($100,000) that was offset to some extent by a couple of timely, sizeable gifts (totaling $55,000) from generous library donors.

The rest of the amount would need to come from journal titles. During 1999-2002 the HAM-TMC Library managed to quadruple its number of electronic journal titles without experiencing more than a handful of cuts to its print subscriptions. Being able to significantly expand electronic access while retaining print subscriptions was partly the result of the Library's fortunate membership in the UT System Digital Library consortium, and partly the result of cost savings achieved in other areas of library operations during the three-year period leading up to 1999.

In identifying titles for possible cancellation, the first approach was to look at the Library's most expensive titles. The Library's subscription agent, Swets Blackwell, was able to provide spreadsheets that easily allowed us to sort titles by cost. Not surprisingly, the 100 most expensive titles (representing less than 5% of the total number of subscriptions) represented approximately 10% of the total budget for serials.

Most, but not all, of these titles were ones that were available both electronically and in print. Most, but not all, titles available electronically were included in packages made available to the HAM-TMC Library through one of its consortial memberships. What were the ramifications of canceling print vs. electronic?

SORTING IT ALL OUT

With print-only titles, the consequences were clear. Canceling a print-only subscription meant that the Library would no longer be providing access to the title (except through interlibrary loan.) Replacing a print subscription with an electronic subscription (if available) would result in no cost savings for the Library. Likewise, there were no savings to be accrued by retaining the electronic version of titles received as part of "print plus electronic" subscriptions through Swets Blackwell, the Library's serials vendor. For savings to occur, both the print and electronic versions of the title would have to go. But what about titles received as part of consortial packages? UTSDL staff members at the University of Texas General Libraries played a critical role in determining the impact various proposed title cuts would have on each package. The results varied significantly according to publisher:

In two different instances the Library identified half a dozen or so expensive to moderately expensive titles it wanted to cut. After consulting with the respective publishers, UTSDL staff reported that the first publisher found the proposed cuts acceptable; they would have no impact on the HAM-TMC Library's continued participation in the consortial arrangement, nor would the Library lose access to any of the titles in the package.

In the other instance, the publisher's response was exactly the opposite. Although the half dozen titles totaling about $6,000 represented less than 10% of the HAM-TMC Library's total expenditures with the publishers, canceling the print to the half dozen in question would result in the Library being ejected from the consortial arrangement, losing access to more than 300 electronic journal titles.

Not surprisingly, the biggest group of high-priced titles on the HAM-TMC Library's tentative cancellation list was also part of the UT System Digital Library's largest consortial package. If the HAM-TMC Library followed through on canceling its 100 most expensive titles, the dollar amount of cancelled titles from this individual publisher would easily exceed the "no more than 1% cancellations per year" system-wide rule included in the consortial agreement. The Library might have to withdraw from the agreement altogether, thereby jeopardizing access to more than 1,000 electronic journals in the publisher's catalog.

ON THE HORNS OF A DILEMMA

What To Do?

Targeting the Library's most expensive titles would achieve the maximum number of dollars with the least disruption in print subscriptions but would have a devastating effect on the offering of electronic journals, reducing them by as much as one-third to one-half, depending on which scenario played out. Looking at print-only subscriptions was equally depressing. The HAM-TMC Library's print-only titles were also, by and large, its least expensive titles. If the Library were to take a hands-off approach to electronic subscriptions, nearly 1,000 print-only journal titles–nearly half the current journals–would need to be eliminated to reach the $150,000 target for reducing expenditures on serials.

In the end, a combination approach was used. Where it was possible to eliminate e-journal subscriptions without losing access to an entire package, we did so. In the case of Wiley Interscience, which had adopted a new pricing mechanism under which 90% of a journal title's cost resided with the electronic version, it was decided to cancel print subscriptions and–for the first time–make the titles available to users on an "e-access only" basis.

Thanks to the intercession of our colleagues at the UT System Digital Library, we were able to negotiate an informal agreement with our largest publisher whereby we canceled a significant number of titles. Although electronic access to these titles was lost, the Library continued to have access to the other titles in the consortial package.

The balance, of course, was made up by a hodge-podge of print only titles or "print plus electronic" titles. In many instances subscriptions to these titles were held by other libraries in the local consortium or by non-medical libraries in the Houston-Galveston area. In the end about 150 titles, worth about $150,000, were processed for cancellation during FY 2002-2003.

What Does It All Mean?

If in the mid to late 1980s, when serials hyperinflation first reared its ugly head, someone had said of the painful cancellation projects going on at the time, "Enjoy it while you can, this is the easy part!" the reaction would have been hysterical, if not homicidal, and yet that's where librarians are today. The advent of electronic resources and more particularly the emergence of bundled "big deal" journal/database packages and consortial purchasing agreements has infinitely complicated the calculus of serials cancellations, a process that has always been the stickiest of wickets.

It is tempting, under the circumstances, to try to "game the system," looking for the one loophole or ideal combination that results in the maximum bang for the buck. Eventually it begins to feel like those of us who deal with serials cancellations are engaged in a giant game of Three Card Monte, the old shell game from the carnival midway.

The ultimate question is: Who's the Rube? The publisher or the librarian?

As libraries devise strategies to cut serials expenditures during times of fiscal exigencies and within the context of bundled e-resources and consortial deals, it is worth remembering, "There's no such thing as free lunch!" The best we are likely to do is come up with a way to share the pain equitably across disciplines and formats.

The Ames Library:
A Model for Collection Integration

Julia B. Dickinson

Sarah E. George

SUMMARY. Illinois Wesleyan University's Ames Library opened in January 2002. The vision for this library focused on creating a user-centered arrangement of information regardless of format. Much of the library's collection was integrated during the move to the new building; however, several discrete collections remain separate. This article will discuss the rationale for the incomplete integration. The authors reflect on the first year's successes, as well as lingering issues, and consider future opportunities for further integration. *[Article copies available for a fee from The Haworth Document Delivery Service: 1-800-HAWORTH. E-mail address: <docdelivery@haworthpress.com> Website: <http://www.HaworthPress.com> © 2006 by The Haworth Press, Inc. All rights reserved.]*

KEYWORDS. Integrated collections, electronic resources, library building planning

---

Julia B. Dickinson is Public Services Librarian (E-mail: jdickins@iwu.edu); and Sarah E. George is Serials Librarian (E-mail: sgeorge@iwu.edu), both at The Ames Library, Illinois Wesleyan University, PO Box 2899, Bloomington, IL 61702.

[Haworth co-indexing entry note]: "The Ames Library: A Model for Collection Integration." Dickinson, Julia B., and Sarah E. George. Co-published simultaneously in *The Acquisitions Librarian* (The Haworth Information Press, an imprint of The Haworth Press, Inc.) No. 35/36, 2006, pp. 167-179; and: *Integrating Print and Digital Resources in Library Collections* (ed: Audrey Fenner) The Haworth Information Press, an imprint of The Haworth Press, Inc., 2006, pp. 167-179. Single or multiple copies of this article are available for a fee from The Haworth Document Delivery Service [1-800-HAWORTH, 9:00 a.m. - 5:00 p.m. (EST). E-mail address: docdelivery@haworthpress.com].

Available online at http://www.haworthpress.com/web/AL
© 2006 by The Haworth Press, Inc. All rights reserved.
Digital Object Identifier: 10.1300/J101v18n35_13

INTRODUCTION

After five short years of planning and construction, Illinois Wesleyan University's Ames Library opened in January 2002. As stated in the *Library Vision Statement* of October 1996, the new library is the place "where scholarly information, regardless of format, is gathered, organized, and prepared for dissemination to the University community." Merging traditional tools of scholarship with information technology formed the foundation of the philosophy of integration for the new facility. The focus on a unified collection required the consolidation of collections in a branch library and storage facility as well as the integration of bibliographic formats.

Illinois Wesleyan University is a private undergraduate institution comprising a College of Liberal Arts, a College of Fine Arts, and a School of Nursing. The University maintains a student body of approximately 2,000. For the past decade, Illinois Wesleyan has concentrated on raising admissions selectivity and academic standards as well as improving physical facilities. An important part of the campus improvements was the construction of a new library. The 103,000 square foot building has five floor levels and houses over 350,000 volumes, 100 public-use computers, and a variety of public space options, including an information commons, an instruction lab, sixteen group study rooms, three project rooms equipped with presentation software and projection equipment, and 150 upholstered lounge chairs and couches. Construction inside The Ames Library was not yet complete when the entire collection, over 25,000 linear feet from three distinct locations, was moved into the new facility in December 2001.

INTEGRATION PHILOSOPHY

Collection integration is not a new concept to libraries. Serials, government documents, and mixed media materials have long been a part of the integration debate with each library addressing its own local needs with regard to the issue. Decisions to integrate formats have been guided by technological advances, space demands, human resource allocations, and user expectations.

As the planning process for the organization of the collection in the new library began, surveys and focus groups were conducted in order to gather feedback about the ways Illinois Wesleyan students and faculty preferred to study, research, teach, and generally use the library. To complement differing needs, a variety of spaces were designed. Study carrels, large tables, group study rooms, and upholstered furniture are all within close proximity to network jacks to allow combined use of print and electronic materials from a single location. By encouraging the interaction of patrons with various formats, the library planners sought to facilitate serendipitous discovery and the development of an individualized relationship with the library. Policies and practices from the old library, such as stand-alone CD-ROM workstations and separate computers designated for word-processing or for research involving networked subscription databases, were eliminated. Divisions among the various uses of the library's resources are continuing to blur. Illinois Wesleyan students often simultaneously search databases, e-mail or chat with professors and classmates, and draft a research paper saved to a shared folder on a campus server. It is in the same spirit of customized multi-tasking that the library staff committed to and embarked upon the creation and provision of a more user-centered integrated collection.

INTEGRATION REALITY

Once the philosophy of the new building had been agreed to, a survey of the current situation was required to assess the readiness of the collection for integration. Materials were considered by format and location. Concerns included cataloging, evaluation, and deselection.

Integration of formats was already apparent in a few places. The circulating collection included books, monographic series, and a few stand-alone CD-ROMs. The online catalog provided electronic access to items owned in print if a URL in the 856 field was already present in the MARC record. A locally created database of journal titles provided a comprehensive list of print, full-text, and electronic journals to which the library had subscriptions. Almost all print subscriptions to indexes and abstracts had been replaced by online databases. A comprehensive list of print and electronic indexes/databases was available on the library's Web page.

With this knowledge, the journal collection was identified as the most significant addition to the integrated collection. At that time journals were located in three places: the periodicals stacks, the Music Library, and an off-site storage facility. It had not been current practice to catalog journals or to assign call numbers to the bound volumes because the journals were arranged alphabetically by title. Because this was such a key component to the integration, it was agreed that cataloging the journals would begin immediately and take precedence over other potential cataloging projects.

At that time there were approximately 2,000 titles that needed attention. For all unbound, non-barcoded journals, summary holdings statements were added to the catalog instead of individual item records. The collection in off-site storage required evaluation before cataloging. This collection contained all journals published before 1987 and included many gift subscriptions that had not been previously processed for the collection. Titles that were unbound, consisted of fewer than five years' worth of issues, or contained content that was outside of the current collection development policy were evaluated for their relevance to the collection. Initial flagging was done by the Serials Librarian, and individual liaisons made final decisions on retention. Overall, one hundred titles were removed from the library's collection.

Many of the journals were loose issues held in Princeton file boxes. This storage method was not conducive to an integrated collection, so a massive bindery project was initiated. Unfortunately, due to staff changes and the load on cataloging, this project was not accomplished before the move. Therefore, Technical Services staff had to go back to the unbound journals and label each Princeton file. The first summer after the move, volumes were sent off for retrospective binding. Approximately 4,000 volumes have been bound and cataloged as the final stages of this project approach. One benefit to this retrospective cataloging and binding project has been the identification of a number of journals that now have electronic counterparts. Many of these links have been added to the library's journal title database.

Before the move, audiovisual media had a separate location. The collection primarily included videos, laser discs, and 16mm films. Items in outdated or less common formats were evaluated, and replacements in common formats (e.g., VHS) were obtained when available. All of these items are now part of the main circulating collection.

The government documents collection had been housed in several different locations. The most heavily used items were cataloged and shelved with the circulating collection. A few legal reference sources in the documents collection were also cataloged, but due to space shortages, these materials were not shelved with the reference collection. The rest of the government documents remained uncataloged. During summer 2001, a major weeding project was initiated so that the focus of the collection could shift from an historical collection to an active, current collection that is more suitable for an undergraduate curriculum. The project identified superseded items and other items that no longer fit the collection focus. Additional steps have included an effort to build depth in the collection, which heavily relies on electronic resources. As depository libraries respond to the increasing trend toward electronic-only materials, the need to distinguish between and enhance access to both print and electronic documents has become paramount.

CD-ROMs had been located in a variety of places depending on their content and use. Deciding where a new acquisition would be located was convoluted and tedious. Those that accompany books were typically cataloged and shelved with the book. When possible, reference-type materials were placed on the network and accessible anywhere within the library. Other CD-ROMs were kept at the Reference Desk for use on one computer, which had the appropriate software loaded. CD-ROMs that came with journals were held until the print journal had been cataloged and then were added to the periodicals stacks with its print counterpart. Integration has simplified the process of locating CD-ROMs because there are two main choices for location–the circulating collection and clusters of scholarly workstations. These workstation clusters are viewed as an extension of the collection and are situated among the shelving units; in effect, spatially merging traditional print tools with digital resources.

The library's collection of microformats included serials on microfilm and microfiche, and the *Early American Imprints* on microcard. The serials had been arranged alphabetically in cabinets. Initially, integrating the microformats into the main collection was considered. This arrangement would allow users access to all of the Library's holdings for a particular title in one place, yet presented significant storage issues. Ultimately, the decision was made to keep the microfilm and microfiche collections together in traditional cabinets. This decision did not, however, eliminate the need for processing the collection. In efforts to keep the collection's arrangement consistent with the rest of the library, microformats needed to be arranged by call number; therefore, each piece had to be labeled before being placed in the cabinets. A separate analysis for the microcard collections showed that the call numbers for this material naturally occurred on the floor designated to house the microfilm reader/printers and that students using this format would most likely receive a formal introduction to these sources by teaching or library faculty. Therefore, the boxes of microcards were integrated with the main collection.

LIMITING FACTORS GOVERNING INTEGRATION

Full integration of the library's collection requires an enormous amount of resources. Most of these resources have limitations, which ultimately forced the process of integration into phases of implementation. For The Ames Library project, there were five major determining factors: a low level of staffing in Technical Services, an integrated library system with certain limitations, an incomplete collection development policy, an aggressive construction timeline, and staff turnover.

An integrated collection requires a higher level of bibliographic control, which the online catalog typically provides. Many of the discrete collections that were housed in the old library were not cataloged, and any consolidation of these collections would first require cataloging and processing the items to fit within LC classification. The library cataloging staff at the beginning of this project included one full-time and two part-time staff members. This number increased to two full-time and one part-time staff members by the time the move into the new library occurred. The current staffing level still hinders the ability to perform original cataloging and, therefore, restricts the number of options in terms of using the online catalog as the sole authority for the library's holdings.

Illinois Wesleyan is part of ILCSO, a consortium of over 50 academic libraries in Illinois. Until summer 2002, the consortium shared one union catalog supported by an ILS system with severe limitations, which significantly influenced Technical Services' workflow and users' accessibility to library resources. Sharing a database with other schools restricted the options for cataloging particular collections, e.g., electronic journals. Additionally, the consortium was expected to and later did change ILS vendors so that there was hesitation to invest much time or effort in making a process work in the old system because the new ILS would provide much more flexibility in cataloging. Another benefit with the new ILS was the decision by the consortium to create a database for each institution.

The library's collection development policy was approved by the University in fall 2000. At that time the building plan had already been approved, and many decisions regarding the collection had already been made. Certain sections of the policy were, in effect, placeholders for verbiage that would be written at a later point. The library staff anticipated the addition of positions whose expertise would be in these areas and who would be responsible for completing these sections of the policy. Collections that were affected included reference and government documents. As such, neither policy for these two discrete collections provided sufficient guidance for selection, retention, and management of print and particularly electronic formats. Having no advocate to envision how these collections might contribute to an integrated collection as a whole, they remained as they were in the old library, separate.

Planning for The Ames Library began in 1996 and proceeded in fits and starts based upon the likelihood of available funding. In fall 1999 the Board of Trustees approved the building of the library, and construction began in the following February. Although many of the big decisions had already been made, revisions to the building plan and additional details were necessary. For example, the original drawings called for a room adjacent to the Information Commons to house the microformat collection and its machines. However, by the time construction began, it was clear that such space would be needed for additional staff offices. This decision then left the microformat collection without a location, and a decision had to be made relatively quickly about its placement so that the furniture prospectus could be revised and sent out for bid. Additionally, the short time span allotted for planning did not allow library staff to incorporate many changes in online resources into the initial wave of opening the new building. By necessity the focus was on the existing print and electronic collection.

In 1998, the library hired a consultant to assist in planning for operation of the new library. The consultant's report recommended a 50% increase in staff levels, to bring the total to nine professional librarians and twelve support positions. These positions would be phased in with the goal of being fully staffed by the opening of the new library. In addition to these new positions, there were two retirements from the professional staff and many other leaves among the professional and support staff due to sabbaticals, one-year visiting appointments, medical leaves, and others. Moreover, by opening day of The Ames Library, only six of twenty-one library employees had participated in the original planning process. Having so many new staff each year required an enormous investment in time for training and getting acclimated to campus. Therefore, the professional expertise that the new hires possessed often did not surface quickly; so many resources had already been devoted to preparations for the new building that it was not possible to accommodate new ideas for integration when they did arise.

DISCRETE COLLECTIONS

Despite the goal of an integrated collection, several discrete collections remain in the new library. The three reasons for this separation are the need for special equipment or assistance to use the collection, uncertainty regarding the long-term relevance of the collection to the general collection, and user behavior.

Many non-print items require special equipment, and the equipment often requires staff support and assistance. The biggest obstacle in integrating the microformat collection was budgetary. The library owned one microfilm reader/printer, and a second machine was included in the equipment budget for the new library. However, an additional two machines would be necessary if there were to be equipment on all floors, and the equipment budget would not support such a purchase. If users needed to move to another floor to find a microfilm reader/printer, then there was less reason to go to the expense of integrating the microfilm with the main collection. Therefore, the microfilm and its equipment were placed on the third floor of the library, where the nearby Music and Media Center could support this collection. The Music and Media Center also supports use of the musical CD and LP collection. The compact discs have been cataloged by accession number and would require additional processing to assign a call number for each disc. The only record players in the building are located in the Center, adjacent to the shelving for the audio materials.

Uncertainty of how a format or material type fits into the long-range goals of the library dictates to what extent that format or type will be integrated. When the library was beginning the transition from print indexes to online databases in the early 1990s, the print materials received the same level of support as they had previously, and a separate virtual "place" was created for organizing the databases. Once the electronic format became dominant, the philosophy shifted to integrate them with print resources. The government documents and map collections are additional examples of the second reason for separation. In the past, access to both collections has been limited due in part to a lack of staff to adequately manage and promote the collection. As the library staff works toward defining a collection development policy for government documents, they will likely become candidates for future integration.

Users often want quick access to certain types of information. The library's entry level floor houses several discrete collections that include general interest items and other browsing materials. Sections include the Current Periodicals, a Newspaper and Popular Reading area, and the

Reference Collection. A similar rationale was used in the development of the library's Web page so that users would have quick access to the most frequently used links.

INTEGRATION ASSESSMENT

How well did we succeed? Now that the library has been open for more than a year and patrons have established use patterns, a program of assessment is in the beginning stages of development. There have been a number of successes and surprises. In general, the evaluation of the decision to integrate the journal collection and the media collection consisting of laser discs, videorecordings, and DVDs with the print collection in the first full year of operation has been primarily anecdotal. The library has seen dramatic and sustained increases in gate counts since the move into the new library. During the first few weeks of opening, the number of visitors to the library nearly tripled compared to a similar time period in the old library. One year later, gate counts showed that the average daily patron count had leveled off at approximately twice the old library's average. Often in the evenings, there is not a single computer workstation or group study room left unoccupied. The continued demand for the group study rooms and the project rooms reflect the prevalence of curricular requirements for students to work and produce a product together. There is a growing expectation that students will incorporate the use of various formats in addition to using technology for the completion of their assignments. Browsing the shelves of an integrated collection does seem to play a part in the growing use of the videotape and DVD collection as students are drawn to an access model based on subject content and not on physical format.

Currently there is interest in analyzing the success of the scholarly workstations. Shelving space was sacrificed in order to situate clusters of six computer workstations loaded with specialized software amidst the corresponding subject-specific print collection. In addition to the unique software accessible from the scholarly workstations, all computers in the library are loaded with Microsoft Office applications. There is still some question whether students return to their favorite library spot regardless of the adjacent collection's subject area. An instruction session for upper level chemistry students conducted not in the instruction lab, but at the scholarly workstation cluster providing access to SciFinder Scholar and ChemDraw, however, resulted in the students' recognition of the true purpose of the scholarly workstation.

Each computer defaults to the library's homepage and provides easy access to subject pages that are designed by librarians and are a bibliography of selected discipline-specific print sources merged with networked subscription databases and appropriate free Internet resources. "One-stop" access to basic study tools and materials designed for advanced research seems to be answering the students' desire for convenience and efficiency.

While students seem to be responding very positively to the integrated collection philosophy, some teaching faculty have voiced concerns. Much of the expressed dissatisfaction from teaching faculty stems from the lack of familiarity with the location of library materials needed in a moment's notice for class instruction. Faculty are frustrated by the fact that videos and journals are now integrated in a collection that spans five floors. In the old library, videotapes occupied a finite number of shelves on the entry level and could be quickly scanned if the exact title was forgotten and the call number unknown; journals were shelved alphabetically making known-item retrieval very simple as well. It remains somewhat unclear as to the true source of this type of concern–having an integrated collection or simply the move into the new facility itself.

Another faculty reaction to the more readily apparent integration of electronic and print materials in the new library is a new twist on an old theme. Academic librarians have been dealing with teaching faculty's misperception of Internet sources for some time and are quite familiar with the assignment stipulation, "Do not use the Internet." On the Illinois Wesleyan campus, a few teaching faculty from various disciplines are requiring that their students bypass digital formats entirely and retrieve "the original print hardcopy." In the authors' experience, it is not uncommon for a student under such mandate to approach the reference desk with a full-text article from JSTOR in hand and inquire about finding the article in the print version of the journal. Obviously library faculty need to place a higher priority on continuing conversations with the teaching faculty who are setting this format criterion in order to establish a better understanding of the learning objectives. Perhaps Internet myths need to be reiterated, and remaining misconceptions about the library's use of the Internet as a tool to enhance access to a pre-selected set of academic-oriented materials dispelled; however, a learning objective to teach students about ways to locate information other than using a computer will require a collaborative approach. Professor and librarian should work together in order to redirect student behavior from their digital comfort zone and refocus their efforts on the actual process of completing the assignment and not on merely turning in the end product.

Users of the music collection have experienced frustrations in locating items previously used in the old library. Operating as a branch library serving a specialized population, the Music Library had its own specific policies and established patterns of user behavior. Becoming part of a centralized system meant that familiarity, convenience, and the personalized notion of "MyLibrary" were diminished. Some School of Music faculty and students often feel that their unique needs are not as well served by non-music library personnel.

Once an assessment plan is implemented, one fact which will surely be tallied as a success, a surprise, and an ongoing debate is that many of the librarians are not content with the current status of the format integration and are pushing for the resolution of difficulties encountered with some of the discrete collections. There are some disciplines suffering from a disconnect between the philosophy of the collection use and organization and the partial integration of print and electronic tools. Both music and chemistry use reference sources for advanced research. However, the Reference Collection is purposely located on the entry level based on the assumption that in most instances reference materials are used as a beginning point and often require librarian mediation in terms of identification and explanation of use for novice library patrons. The music and chemistry collections reside on the third and fourth floors, respectively, impeding the ability of students and faculty to use the discipline-specific circulating print collection and electronic tools in conjunction with the advanced reference sources. In order to partially address this problem, an investigation of the replacement of print reference tools with their digital counterparts for these two disciplines is needed.

NEXT STEPS

The philosophy of integration and the actuality of the library's move dictated the initial phases of integration. The next phase of integration will be dictated by user behavior and will focus on enhancing access to the current collection.

The first step is the redesign of the library's Web pages. Although the current pages were designed with the philosophy of "access to information regardless of format" in mind, use of the pages has demonstrated the need for improved and simplified access. Advances in technology will enable better integration of print and electronic resources and coordination of interdisciplinary resources.

In particular, the library staff plans to implement an OpenURL server. It is the librarians' belief that this kind of technology is an important step in navigating the world of information. It will provide a better interface for locating journal articles based upon known citations compared to the current FileMakerPro journal database. OpenURL technology will also bring together the collection and services and facilitate the user's movement to interlibrary loan or reference assistance.

Additionally, the library is pursuing options for purchasing MARC records for collections that are currently not represented in the online catalog. The first set of records will likely be for electronic and full-text journals. However, it is expected that this project would ultimately include electronic books and government documents. Adding these records to the online catalog maintains the library catalog as the official record of the library's holdings and simplifies the user's experience of finding what the library owns or has access to.

As mentioned earlier, the new library's equipment budget included the purchase of a digital microformat reader/scanner. The state-of-the-art scanner functions to unify yet one more format with the digital realm by allowing students to move beyond merely printing microform images toward integrating them within their own individual academic projects. The digital reader/scanner also facilitates desktop delivery of microfilmed content through e-mail and other electronic document format extensions, such as pdf and tiff, so that electronic reserves and interlibrary loan services may benefit from added flexibility with this format as well.

CONCLUSION

The philosophy of access to information regardless of format has become a solid foundation for every endeavor in The Ames Library. The process by which the library staff have been able to achieve the first phase of implementation has reinforced conventional wisdom:

- Deal with what you have before moving on and make sure that the first phase of integration is successful before including additional collections or formats.

- Staff support of a phased implementation is crucial. Consistent communication during the entire project encourages ongoing support from library staff for the current and future phases.
- Limiting factors are not always negative–they can have positive implications. For example, changes in technology may facilitate a better or quicker project in the future.
- Integration benefits the user–not, generally, the library staff or their workflow.

Integrating Resources
in the Education Library:
Trends, Issues, and Reality

Justina O. Osa

SUMMARY. Resources found in the typical education library that supports teacher education programs often include print and non-print library items, and other items that are unique to education library collections. This article attempts to share what the education library is doing to integrate all of its resources irrespective of their formats. The main focus is a description of the two major ways education librarians attempt to integrate library resources. Electronic or online integration is being achieved through the enhancement of local records in the online public access catalog (OPAC). How the education library is physically integrating its collection is also discussed. The challenges and limitations of integration efforts are briefly touched upon. *[Article copies available for a fee from The Haworth Document Delivery Service: 1-800-HAWORTH. E-mail address: <docdelivery@haworthpress.com> Website: <http://www.HaworthPress.com> © 2006 by The Haworth Press, Inc. All rights reserved.]*

Justina O. Osa is Education and Behavioral Sciences Librarian, University Libraries, The Pennsylvania State University, E502-C Paterno Library, University Park, PA 16802-1809 (E-mail: joo2@psulias.psu.edu).

[Haworth co-indexing entry note]: "Integrating Resources in the Education Library: Trends, Issues, and Reality." Osa, Justina O. Co-published simultaneously in *The Acquisitions Librarian* (The Haworth Information Press, an imprint of The Haworth Press, Inc.) No. 35/36, 2006, pp. 181-194; and: *Integrating Print and Digital Resources in Library Collections* (ed: Audrey Fenner) The Haworth Information Press, an imprint of The Haworth Press, Inc., 2006, pp. 181-194. Single or multiple copies of this article are available for a fee from The Haworth Document Delivery Service [1-800-HAWORTH, 9:00 a.m. - 5:00 p.m. (EST). E-mail address: docdelivery@haworthpress.com].

Available online at http://www.haworthpress.com/web/AL
© 2006 by The Haworth Press, Inc. All rights reserved.
Digital Object Identifier: 10.1300/J101v18n35_14

KEYWORDS. Education library, access to information, electronic integration, physical integration, education library collection, local records enhancement, library catalogs, library technical processes

Once upon a time the library housed mainly a collection of written and printed materials. As far back as 1993 it was observed that the contents of libraries had changed so much through the years that the word library itself is, in a sense, inaccurate. The word library comes from the Latin word "liber," which means "books" (*The World Book Encyclopedia* 235). Today a library has to collect information in a variety of formats including print, electronic (online and digital), and three-dimensional materials. The expanded definition of "library" as a repository of information presented in an increasingly wide variety of formats is gaining or has already gained precedence over the narrower meaning of "library" as solely a repository of books. The library collection is now being defined to include both the materials a library owns and those materials to which the library has purchased access. The issue of access is very significant to librarians. They have from time immemorial been preoccupied with the issue of organizing library materials for easy identification, access, and retrieval. Librarians place a high premium on providing patrons with quick and easy access to materials acquired.

INTEGRATING THE COLLECTION–WHAT DO WE MEAN?

It is definitely stating the obvious to say that technology, especially Web technology, has revolutionized what the library collects and how it provides access to information. Black observed that "the impact of the Internet, developments in multi-media, and increasingly sophisticated imaging technology and techniques now being developed have propelled the digital library into a reality that is virtual in nature but concrete in impact" (Black 139). Everywhere in society, technology has immensely accelerated the ease and pace of service delivery. The attraction of the electronic often seduces patrons into believing that everything they need for their research and assignment completion is and should be accessible electronically. Patrons are used to having microwave-fast services and access and they expect the same convenience, quick services, and instantaneous results from the library. Librarians understand the changing desires and needs of their patrons, including their need for one-stop shopping in a seamless electronic environment.

Patrons do not want to be "ping-ponged" from one place to another in search of the information they need, even when the information is packaged in different media.

As previously stated, the library builds collections that contain materials in various formats. Patrons are not really interested in the challenges the library encounters in dealing with resources in different formats. Patrons are demanding quick and easy access to all resources. This patron demand has made the library seek intelligent means of providing quick and convenient access to all of the resources the library has on a subject or a concept. Integration of collections has become a major solution to this challenge. The concept of integration of formats is perceived as a strategy to provide one-stop access to the wide range of heterogeneous materials. This article attempts to focus on the trends, issues, and the reality of integrating education library collections.

LITERATURE REVIEW

Integration of collections which are in a variety of formats could be a challenge to librarians who are committed to organizing knowledge in logical ways and to bringing order out of chaos. "Properly combining library resources to function collectively as a cohesive, efficient unit is the basis of information integration" (Brooks 316). Patrons place a high premium on convenience and online accessibility of resources. They would like the ability to pull together electronically, in a single search, all information the library has on a subject or a concept they are interested in, irrespective of the format in which the information is stored. The library online public access catalog (OPAC) has become a prime medium for the integration of library collections, irrespective of the variety of formats. Consequently, the capabilities, special features, and the level to which a system can be adapted to the needs of a particular library become crucial. When a library is considering a library automation system to purchase there are some pertinent questions about what Brooks termed "behind the scenes" functions which are often asked. Some of these questions include:

- Can we link to our Web-based Online Public Access Catalogs (OPAC) for the most detailed holdings information?
- Can we add "notes" to the database with regard to specific journals?
- Can we customize the search pages?

- Can we choose appropriate search limiters and search expanders?
- Can we choose default search screens?
- Can we establish different methods of user authentication, including remote?
- Can we link from our full-text databases to our collection of e-journals (Brooks 318)?

Levy and Marshall raise additional questions:

> The continuing use of paper and other nondigital materials challenges us to effect a rich integration of media. How must our protocols, our naming schemes, our search procedures be broadened if some of the references [and other library materials] are not–and will never be–in digital form! How must our document architectures be modified to accommodate hybrid documents, parts of which are in digital form while others are on paper? (Levy and Marshall 82)

Despite the fact that, in the case of the education library, some resources are in formats other than digital and paper, patrons still desire fast and easy access.

EDUCATION LIBRARY COLLECTIONS

Education library collections exist to support teacher education programs. The main goal of the education librarian is to acquire and make available resources that assist

1. faculty of the college, school, or department of education to help prospective teachers develop the professional knowledge and skills they need to succeed in the everyday classroom environment, and
2. prospective teachers to package and to repackage the same learning materials in different ways to create learning environments that foster active learning for all students and to promote success for all irrespective of their peculiar characteristics or exceptionalities.

Therefore, education library collections that support teacher education programs must be made up of those resources that have the potential to:

- greatly increase teacher education students' deep understanding of the curriculum and instruction,
- enable them to apply their knowledge to present the contents of lessons in a fashion that makes it possible for all students to learn successfully, irrespective of their learning styles and past experiences,
- help them create a more personalized learning environment where students are actively involved and take responsibility for their own learning.

Building such collections is a tall task for the education librarian. Such collections include textbooks, monographs, periodicals, audio cassettes, video cassettes, microforms, films, posters and charts, realia, kits, dioramas, online databases, preparatory certification materials, music scores, slides, manuscripts, locally created digital items, puppets, flash cards, instructional games, instructional materials, rock collections, models, flat pictures, manipulatives, transparencies, dolls, artifacts, clothing, big books, and musical instruments. Formats may include print, sound recording, motion picture, video recording, electronic resource, kit, text, and visual projection. Integrating materials in all of these different formats constitutes a unique dimension in the task of the education librarian.

WHAT THE EDUCATION LIBRARY IS DOING TO INTEGRATE ITS COLLECTIONS

The concept of integrating resources means pulling all resources together from different sources and making them accessible quickly and easily. Integration of the collection can be done electronically and physically.

Technology has transformed the world of information. It has also changed how users obtain the information they need. Integration of collections without regard to format or location can be accomplished technically to some extent, through the collaboration of subject librarians or specialists, technical services librarians, and the availability of access mechanisms such as *Silverlinker*.

The cataloging department has a crucial role to play in the library's efforts to integrate collections. Catalogers prepare the bibliographic records that are loaded into the searchable OPAC database. The Web-based OPAC serves as the single gateway to almost all resources, including full-text resources in all formats. Some catalogers are more comfortable processing traditional formats such as print. As Urbanski noted, "There is usually good LC (Library of Congress) or bibliographic utility member cataloging for most commercially produced media" (Freeborn, "Retrospective Conversion Cataloging," 5).

The uniqueness of the audience for which the materials are being cataloged continues to be a major consideration as catalogers adopt and adapt the bibliographic records found in commercial sources such as OCLC databases. Catalogers have to "massage" existing bibliographic records to make them fit the classification and cataloging guidelines of their libraries. Catalogers find themselves dealing with more problematic situations when it comes to processing less traditional materials, especially non-print materials such as realia, kits, dioramas, online databases, locally created digital items, locally assembled units, puppets, models, manipulatives, dolls, artifacts, clothing, and multimedia–resources with multiple formats. Freeborn referred to Lynne Howarth's keynote speech at the Online Audiovisual Catalogers 1998 Conference. ("Cataloging of the Weird," 1). Howarth's observation expresses well the problems with preparing full-level bibliographic records for the resources in non-traditional formats which are commonly found in the education library. She said "(1) They're 'different' from standard print materials; (2) Because of this difference, they're 'difficult' to catalog; and (3) They 'divert' cataloging time and resources" (Freeborn, "Cataloging of the Weird," 1).

The job of catalogers is made easier when they are able to locate the record for the item in the union catalog. Sometimes they have to start with a bibliographic record they can locate and modify it to meet their needs. When catalogers fail to locate records for items on the union catalog they must produce original records. They may need to be resourceful and use sophisticated cataloging and classification skills to catalog fully all of the materials the education library acquires, even when the union catalog fails to provide a bibliographic record. They may use the 300, 500, 600 and 800 MARC fields creatively to present more accurate description of items and to provide more access points to items.

ENHANCEMENT OF LOCAL RECORDS

The introduction of the 856 MARC field allows direct linking to the full text of electronic resources. "The 856 field provides an array of possibilities for linking the cataloging record to a variety of relevant sites"

(Bordeianu, Carter, and Dennis 113). From the 856 field in the MARC record in the OPAC database, hotlinks can now be created to provide direct links to resources on the Web or to information stored in any online media. Access mechanisms allow the library to link information seamlessly from multiple user interfaces through the online public catalog. As Bordeianu, Carter, and Dennis stated, because "the 856 field is repeatable it is possible to add additional 856 fields in records as a local enhancement, to link to Web resources that are not part of that bibliographic entity but that could be of significant interest to the patron" (113). Sometimes the knowledge and skills needed to locate such resources go beyond traditional cataloging competencies, requiring knowledge of external resources which are not typically associated with cataloging skills. Such knowledge and skills also overlap with selection and public service expertise (Bordeianu, Carter, and Dennis 113). This is one of the reasons a partnership forged between catalogers, public service librarians, and subject specialists/librarians greatly enhances local bibliographic records. Collaboratively they can enhance and expand the cataloging record to accomplish what would once have been unfathomable. Non-catalogers are good at identifying and pulling together resources on a subject from all sorts of sources and in all sorts of formats, and can be helpful in choosing subject headings under which patrons are most likely to search for resources. Catalogers and non-catalogers must work together at distinguishing the content of the item because subject analysis is a crucial source for deriving access points.

Once catalogers have relevant information on resources, they use their expertise to provide links and pointers from one bibliographic record to another and to cross reference resources. In addition to the 856 field, some Web-based OPACs are beginning to make other MARC fields linkable, a development that increases the flexibility of the local record. Some libraries index the 500 field to generate more access points to their resources. Web technology has made the possibilities almost limitless.

Catalogers describe each electronic resource as a distinct entry. Examples of such electronic resources include: Web-based journals and aggregated databases, stable and free electronic resources, and online free teacher certification examination preparation materials. Bibliographic records are created at full-level cataloging. Each record describes an item, classifies it, and assigns a call number. The URL that has the capability to link the patron directly to the electronic resource is provided in the record. Merely clicking on the URL gives a patron access to the full text of the item.

The Web-based OPAC has become the centralized source of access to all resources in all formats. Currently, a patron can perform a single search of the online catalog and retrieve a combination of resources in different formats. For example, when a patron performs a keyword search at Paterno Library for materials on "teaching language," he/she retrieves different types of resources in different formats. A sampling of items in the result list includes:

- *Muzzy. Level II. French*–a kit which includes 4 videocassettes, 1 computer optical disc, 2 sound cassettes, 1 activity masters, 1 teacher's guide, and 1 year of lesson plans.
- *Working with Words and Images: New Steps in an Old Dance*–a book.
- *Los Días de la Semana*–a poster.
- *Teacher's Manual and Answer Book, Hayes Exercises in English*, grade six–a textbook.
- *Teach Me More–Chinese [sound recording]: [A Musical Journey through the Year]*–a sound disc and a book.
- *National Geographic Italian* [electronic resource]–three computer optical discs and a phrase book.
- *Pedagogy (Online)*–Project Muse. Electronic Journal–an electronic journal.

The search screen is now designed and configured in such a way that patrons are able to specify the types of resources and formats they desire. Often limiters help to refine the search and make it more focused and specific, given the information needs of the patron who is performing the search. For example, the limiter "material type" allows a patron to search specifically for formats such as manuscripts, CD-ROMs and other digital formats, instructional materials, juvenile books, fiction, non-fiction, picture books, video material, musical scores, maps, kits, microforms, microfiche, multimedia, and online resources.

DISPLAY OF SEARCH RESULTS

The items or "hits" included in the result list are displayed in a brief titles list, where the general material designation (GMD) is indicated. When the patron clicks on a "detail" button he/she is taken to a single item display screen. For example, when a patron clicks on the detail button for *Learn Russian Now*! he/she is told the item is an electronic resource, and in the 300 field he/she is given the physical description of the item: 1 computer optical disc :|bsd., col. ;|c4 3/4 in. +|e1 bonus CD with insert (4 3/4 in.) + 1 booklet insert (8 p. ; 12 cm.).

In the case of *Pedagogy (Online)*–Project Muse–electronic journal, a hyperlink (http://www.lias.psu.edu/scripts/linklias.exe?where=Go+There&what=MUSE) has been inserted into the bibliographic record on the single item display screen. This bibliographic record contains linking fields to the full text, and patrons can easily click their way to the full text of the journal article. Though the patrons do not have instantaneous access to the item on the single item display screen, they prefer the option of extra clicking on the hyperlink to access the full text or the full image version of the information, to the option of writing down the bibliographic citation correctly, physically getting up from the computer chair, walking or riding the elevator to the floor where the paper copy of the journal is housed, trying to understand the floor plan so as to know the direction to go, locating the call number range, identifying the particular volume, and turning the pages to find the article. If the patron needs a copy of the article in an online journal or from a full-text database, he/she would only have to click to send the print command. Patrons now have the additional option of e-mailing the full text of an electronic journal to themselves or to anyone else. But if the article is available only in print format, the patron will have to go to the stacks, get the volume, locate a photocopier, and copy the article page by page.

PHYSICAL INTEGRATION

Integration of collections could be understood as providing a one-stop electronic access to all resources in all formats, and also as interfiling them physically on the shelf irrespective of formats. When library items and information sources on a subject or concept are interfiled and are physically shelved together in one location on the shelf, advantages include:

1. patrons have enhanced and easier access to these sources and
2. patrons can chance upon some useful information they did not set out to look for by browsing the shelves.

To some extent the collection in an education library could be inter-shelved so that all materials about a subject or on a concept could sit side by side on the shelf. There is usually little problem interfiling traditional print materials on the same subject or concept and placing them side by side on the shelf. The challenge comes when one has to deal with the shelving of non-traditional library materials. Given the nature of the materials found in the education library, one finds items that are unusual in terms of shape, size, and texture. Some of the items consist of multiple parts that are of different materials and are in different formats.

HOW THE EDUCATION LIBRARY INTEGRATES MATERIALS PHYSICALLY

Access is important to education librarians but they have to be realistic and execute a shelving plan that is feasible and that makes sense. During the material selection process format is not allowed to influence collection acquisition decisions adversely. On the contrary, materials in formats that could be considered unusual by non-education librarians may actually be the feature that positively influenced the acquisition decision. It is believed that when students are actively involved in their own learning, effective learning is achieved. Resources which often come in non-standard formats, shapes, texture, and size have been found to greatly enhance learning for all children, especially those who are at risk of being left behind. Teacher education students are taught and encouraged to integrate such resources creatively into their instructional activities so that every student is enabled to learn irrespective of their learning styles, past experiences, and peculiar characteristics. Therefore education librarians value these materials and process them creatively, purchasing special containers and special shelving to house them.

When new materials are received in the education library, processing begins. The materials are carefully examined and analyzed. They are sorted, classified, and assigned subject headings that will help pull together all resources that could be of interest to the same patron. To illustrate the point, here is an example. Five titles arrived for the Education Library at Paterno 5th Floor:

GeoSafari Electronic Learning Game

The Story of Rock Music

World History

Learn Basic English

Sports Pages

Upon careful examination it became clear that these titles belong together and therefore should be shelved together. All five are to be used with the *GeoSafari Electronic Learning Game,* and the bibliographic record should reflect all five items.

The education librarian and catalogers collaborated to assign a call number that would pull these five items together and make them physically adjacent on the shelf. If these five items were cataloged individually, the following call numbers would be assigned to them:

GeoSafari Electronic Learning Game–G3201.S73E4 1995

The Story of Rock Music–ML3534.S76 1996

World History–D21.1.W67 1993

Learn Basic English–PE1128.A2L42 1993

Sports Pages–GV571.S58 1996

It was decided that the best way to keep all the materials together was to give them all the same base call number. The class number LB1029 for educational games was chosen and the Cutter number G46 for *Geosafari* was added. Consequently the base call number to be used was LB1029.G3G46.

Identifying the individual item was the next issue to be dealt with. Location codes were added that would help pull similar items together on the shelf. For example, for *The Story of Rock Music,* "musicr" was chosen. For *World History,* "historyw" was chosen. The final result was that those five items were assigned the following call numbers:

GeoSafari Electronic Learning Game–LB1029.G3G46 1995

The Story of Rock Music–LB1029.G3G46 musicr 1996

World History–LB1029.G3G46 historyw 1993

Learn Basic English–LB1029.G3G46 englishb 1993

Sports Pages–LB1029.G3G46 sports 1996

When an item comes with multiple parts, in different formats, shapes, and sizes the subject content and intended use of the item determine how it is treated. Here are two examples of this group of materials.

Example 1:

245: Volcanoes, earthquakes and tsunamis|h[kit]

300: 1 activity guide (8 p. : ill. ; 22 cm.), 24 experiment cards, 3 identical copies of map of continental drift, ping pong ball, 5 balloons, magnifying lens, sandpaper, 5 metal washers, 3 volcanic rocks, plastic ruler|cin container 23 × 9 × 15 cm.

The parts that constitute this item, *Volcanoes, Earthquakes and Tsunamis*, are in print and non-print, and are made of paper, plastic, metal, rubber, and rock. The multiple parts are in different shapes and sizes. Because they are intended to be used together, all of the parts must be shelved together for easy access and use. The container that enables the library to put these heterogeneous items together does not readily lend itself to being interfiled with monographs in the collection.

Example 2:

245: Our amazing solar system|h[kit] : |bplanetary science kit.

300: 16 snap-together plastic halves, 4 plastic ring disks, 1 sculpey modeling compound, 1 model gauge, 1 sandpaper, 8 containers of non-toxic paint, 2 paint brushes, 1 sponge, 1 painting guide, 4 stands (with 4 mounting posts, moon arm, and labels), 1 package (with thread, nylon line, adhesive square, and paper clips), 1 sun poster, and 1 science book; |cin container 33 × 36 × 7 cm.

The parts that constitute this item, *Our Amazing Solar System*, are in print and non-print, and are made of paper, modeling clay, cellulose, acrylic, plastic, metal, rubber, thread, and liquid. The multiple parts are in different shapes and sizes. All parts must be shelved together for easy access and use because all are needed to construct a fully 3-dimensional scale model of the solar system, including all nine planets, the principal moons, planetary rings, and a full-color sun poster. Interfiling such a kit into the monograph or periodical collections would not be physically possible.

Some educational materials with only one piece do not easily lend themselves to physical integration into the usual book collection. Examples of such items include *The Tooth Model*, which is 61 × 45 × 7 cm. in size, and *The Ear Model*, which measures 32 × 40 × 19 cm.

ISSUES/CHALLENGES AND THE FUTURE

There are limitations to the integration efforts of the library. There are still some locally networked resources that are not integrated into the main mechanism of resource location and retrieval. Catalogers' workload has greatly increased because of the increasingly higher demand being placed on them to design ways to utilize fully the ever rising possibilities and functionalities which Web technology is offering. Cataloging rules do not seem applicable to all of the special circumstances catalogers encounter daily as they try to meet the expectations and needs of users. Sometimes catalogers find themselves massaging cataloging rules and working around them to accomplish their purpose. It has become difficult to integrate and use some records contributed to national cataloging utilities, and catalogers may need to make local modifications.

The level to which the library can link is based to a large extent on the vendor's willingness and cooperation. Copyright sometimes keeps librarians from providing direct access to some resources such as LPs and CD-ROMs, and from undertaking dramatic digital projects. A united voice from librarians may help the integration venture. The power of the marketplace may encourage vendors, library system developers and others in the information business to develop and deliver resources without added layers of complication so that users can access all resources easily and quickly, with as few steps as possible. In spite of the issues and challenges librarians encounter, progress is being made in integration efforts.

CONCLUSION

The education library acquires items and resources that support instructional programs. These materials store or present information in a wide variety of different formats, yet format or medium must not present an obstacle to access.

This article has discussed two main strategies for integrating materials in library collections: electronic and physical. A Web-based OPAC is the primary locator and gateway to resources in all formats. The enhancement of local records has greatly propelled the library forward in its integration efforts. Hyperlinks inserted into bibliographic records make direct access to full text easy and fast.

As much as librarians would like to integrate collections fully, the nature of the items in the education library poses some challenges. Some items cannot be placed physically side by side with other materials that cover the same subjects or concepts. The size, shape and number of pieces that make up items influence shelving decisions. In the education library, electronic integration may be easier to achieve than physical integration.

REFERENCES

Black, Graham. "Integrating the Digital with the Non-Digital: A Librarian's Perspective." *Proceedings of ISDL '95* (1995): 138-44. 11 March 2003. <http://www.dl.ulis.ac.jp/ISDL95/proceedings/pages75/138.html>.

Bordeianu, Sever, Christina E. Carter, and Nancy K. Dennis. "Delivering Electronic Resources with Web OPACs and Other Web-based Tools: Needs of Reference Librarians." *Reference Services Review* 28.2. (2000): 111-18.

Brooks, Sam. "Integration of Information Resources and Collection Development Strategy." *The Journal of Academic Librarianship* 27.4 (2001): 316-19.

Freeborn, Robert B. "Cataloging of the Weird: Further Examples for the 3-D Perplexed." *MC Journal: The Journal of Academic Media Librarianship* 6.2 (1999): 1-6. 19 March 2003. <http://wings.buffalo.edu/publications/mcjrnl/v6n2/freeborn.html>.

_____. "Retrospective Conversion Cataloging of Audiovisual Materials at Penn State University's Education Library." *MC Journal: The Journal of Academic Media Librarianship* 7.1 (2000): 5-8. 21 February 2003. <http://wings.buffalo.edu/publications/mcjrnl/v7n1/freeborn.html>.

Levy, David M., and Catherine C. Marshall. "Going Digital: A Look at Assumptions Underlying Digital Libraries." *Communications of the ACM* 38.4 (1995): 78-84.

"Library." *The World Book Encyclopedia.* 1997 ed.

Index

© 2006 by The Haworth Press, Inc. All rights reserved.

BOOK ORDER FORM!

Order a copy of this book with this form or online at:
http://www.HaworthPress.com/store/product.asp?sku=5519

Integrating Print and Digital Resources
in Library Collections

_____ in softbound at $29.95 ISBN-13: 978-0-7890-2834-1 / ISBN-10: 0-7890-2834-4.
_____ in hardbound at $49.95 ISBN-13: 978-0-7890-2833-4 / ISBN-10: 0-7890-2833-6.

COST OF BOOKS _____

POSTAGE & HANDLING _____
US: $4.00 for first book & $1.50
for each additional book
Outside US: $5.00 for first book
& $2.00 for each additional book.

SUBTOTAL _____

In Canada: add 7% GST. _____

STATE TAX _____
CA, IL, IN, MN, NJ, NY, OH, PA & SD residents
please add appropriate local sales tax.

FINAL TOTAL _____
If paying in Canadian funds, convert
using the current exchange rate,
UNESCO coupons welcome.

❏ BILL ME LATER:
Bill-me option is good on US/Canada/
Mexico orders only; not good to jobbers,
wholesalers, or subscription agencies.

❏ Signature _____

❏ Payment Enclosed: $ _____

❏ PLEASE CHARGE TO MY CREDIT CARD:

❏ Visa ❏ MasterCard ❏ AmEx ❏ Discover
❏ Diner's Club ❏ Eurocard ❏ JCB

Account # _____

Exp Date _____

Signature _____

(Prices in US dollars and subject to change without notice.)

PLEASE PRINT ALL INFORMATION OR ATTACH YOUR BUSINESS CARD

Name

Address

City   State/Province   Zip/Postal Code

Country

Tel   Fax

E-Mail

May we use your e-mail address for confirmations and other types of information? ❏ Yes ❏ No We appreciate receiving
your e-mail address. Haworth would like to e-mail special discount offers to you, as a preferred customer.
We will never share, rent, or exchange your e-mail address. We regard such actions as an invasion of your privacy.

Order from your **local bookstore** or directly from
The Haworth Press, Inc. 10 Alice Street, Binghamton, New York 13904-1580 • USA
Call our toll-free number (1-800-429-6784) / Outside US/Canada: (607) 722-5857
Fax: 1-800-895-0582 / Outside US/Canada: (607) 771-0012
E-mail your order to us: orders@HaworthPress.com

For orders outside US and Canada, you may wish to order through your local
sales representative, distributor, or bookseller.
For information, see http://HaworthPress.com/distributors

(Discounts are available for individual orders in US and Canada only, not booksellers/distributors.)

The Haworth Press Inc.

Please photocopy this form for your personal use.
www.HaworthPress.com

BOF05